8-25-2024
To: My Beautiful S

STUD
DELIVERANCE
— MADE EASY —

May God Bless you everyday.!
Let's never give up!

from: Violet

STUDY GUIDE
DELIVERANCE
—MADE EASY—

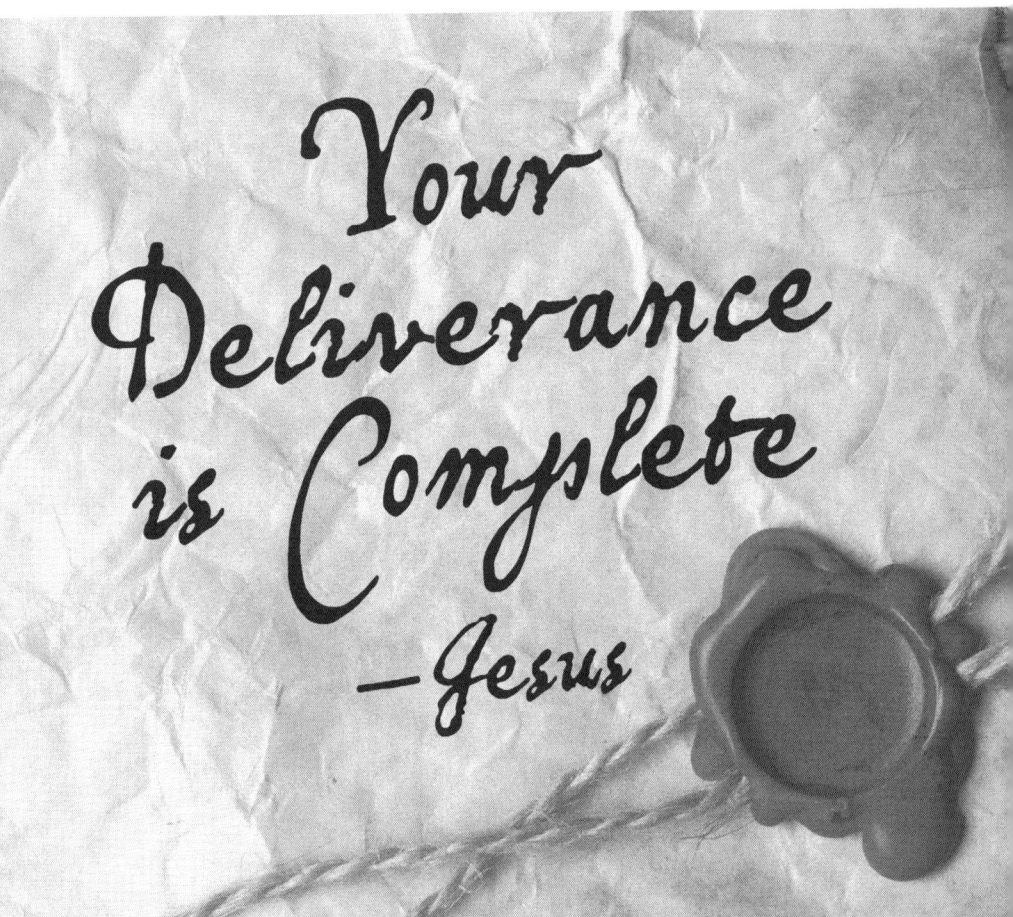

Dr. Kevin L. Zadai

© Copyright 2024 Kevin L. Zadai.

All rights reserved. This book is protected by the copyright laws of the United States of America. This book may not be copied or reprinted for commercial gain or profit. The use of short quotations or the copying of an occasional page for personal or group study is permitted and encouraged. Permission will be granted upon request.

Unless otherwise indicated, Scripture quotations are taken from the New King James Version. Copyright © 1982 by Thomas Nelson, Inc. Used by permission. All rights reserved.

All Scripture quotations marked (KJV) are taken from the King James Version. Public Domain.

Scripture quotations marked (NLT) are taken from the Holy Bible, New Living Translation, copyright ©1996, 2004, 2015 by Tyndale House Foundation. Used by permission of Tyndale House Publishers, a Division of Tyndale House Ministries, Carol Stream, Illinois 60188. All rights reserved.

Scripture quotations marked (ESV) are taken from the English Standard Version, Copyright © 2001 by Crossway, a publishing ministry of Good News Publishers. All rights reserved.

Scripture quotations marked (AMP) are taken from the Amplified Bible, Copyright © 1954, 1958, 1962, 1964, 1965, 1987 by The Lockman Foundation. Used by permission. www.Lockman.org.

Scripture quotations marked (TPT) are from The Passion Translation®. Copyright © 2017, 2018 by Passion & Fire Ministries, Inc. Used by permission. All rights reserved. www.thePassionTranslation.com.

Please note that Warrior Notes publishing style capitalizes certain pronouns in Scripture that refer to the Father, Son, and Holy Spirit, which may differ from some publishers' styles. Take note that the name "satan" and related names are not capitalized. We choose not to acknowledge him, even to the point of violating accepted grammatical rules. The author and Warrior Notes have made an intentional decision to italicize many Scriptures in block quotes.

Warrior Notes Publishing

P O Box 1288

Destrehan, LA 70047

Cover design: Virtually Possible Designs

For more information about our school, go to www.warriornotesschool.com. Reach us on the internet: www.Kevinzadai.com

ISBN 13 TP: 978-1-6631-0094-8

ISBN 13 eBook: 978-1-6631-0095-5

DEDICATION

I dedicate this book to the Lord Jesus Christ. When I died during surgery and met with Jesus on the other side, He insisted that I return to life on the earth and that I help people with their destinies. Because of Jesus' love and concern for people, the Lord has actually chosen to send a person back from death to help everyone who will receive that help so that his or her destiny and purpose is secure in Him.

I want You, Lord, to know that when You come to take me to be with You someday, it is my sincere hope that people remember not me, but the revelation of Jesus Christ that You have revealed through me. I want others to know that I am merely being obedient to Your heavenly calling and mission, which is to reveal Your plan for the fulfillment of the divine destiny for each of God's children.

ACKNOWLEDGMENTS

In addition to sharing my story with everyone through the book *Heavenly Visitation: A Guide to the Supernatural*, God has commissioned me to write over sixty books and study guides. Most recently, the Lord gave me the commission to produce this study guide, *Deliverance Made Easy*. This study guide addresses some of the revelations concerning the areas that Jesus reviewed and revealed to me through the Word of God and by the Spirit of God during several visitations. I want to thank everyone who has encouraged me, assisted me, and prayed for me during the writing of this work. Special thanks to my wonderful wife, Kathi, for her love and dedication to the Lord and me. Thank you to my excellent staff for the wonderful job editing this book. Special thanks as well to all my friends who know about *Deliverance Made Easy* and how to operate in this for the next move of God's Spirit!

CONTENTS

Introduction		11
Chapter 1	The Origin of Spiritual Warfare	13
Chapter 2	The Enemy's Covert Operation	29
Chapter 3	Parameters of Spiritual Authority	43
Chapter 4	The Battle for Your Mind	61
Chapter 5	The Truth Sets Captives Free	77
Chapter 6	Old Testament Framework for Deliverance	95
Chapter 7	Jesus Paid for Your Freedom	107
Chapter 8	The Battle Is Already Won	121
Chapter 9	The Lord's Angelic Army	135
Chapter 10	God Is Your Deliverer	151
Salvation Prayer		169
About Dr. Kevin Zadai		173

Introduction

Deliverance is a subject that many modern-day ministries have made complicated. Yet the truth is that it is very simple once you understand what you are contending with. With the authority given through Jesus Christ, every believer is called to walk in permanent freedom and minister to others. Deliverance was never intended to be a specialized ministry for the spiritually elite, but it should be our lifestyle in the body of Christ.

In this study guide, we will explore Scriptures that reveal how spiritual warfare originated, the victory that has already been won, and how to deal with the enemy daily in every situation you encounter. My prayer is that you become well-versed in this topic and see powerful results in your own life. As you receive the revelation that deliverance is easy, I believe you will also help set many people free and teach them to understand this spiritual battle we are in.

Blessings,

Dr. Kevin L. Zadai

CHAPTER 1

THE ORIGIN OF SPIRITUAL WARFARE

And He said to them, "I saw satan fall like lightning from heaven. Behold, I give you the authority to trample on serpents and scorpions, and over all the power of the enemy, and nothing shall by any means hurt you."
—Luke 10:18–19

DISCUSSION:

The Lord instructed me to write this book to bring understanding of the dynamics of deliverance. Many people do not understand how demons operate both in the lives of believers and nonbelievers. Although I will give a brief overview of the history of satan and the origins of demons, that will not be the focus of this work. This writing aims to equip you to practically execute victory over the unseen enemy you deal with daily. Just as Jesus and His disciples drove out demons, every believer is called to operate in deliverance.

As far as scholars know, satan was a guardian cherub in the Garden of Eden (Ezekiel 28:13–19). We will not go into detail about his origin; the focus will be on how spiritual warfare became an issue with people. The battle started in the garden (Genesis 3); then Genesis 6 shows us what happened afterward. Understanding how the enemy operates behind the scenes is crucial when dealing with daily situations.

The body of Christ struggles with an overwhelming misunderstanding concerning the operation of demonic spirits. I will highlight specific Scriptures to reveal some truths you may not know. Demons are fallen hybrid spirits who are evil, stubborn, and covert. They do not like to be obvious because if exposed, you can effectively deal with them so that they can no longer operate. So they are careful not to reveal their position unless they have to. If you are a threat to them, you may have experiences that others will not.

SONS OF GOD AND DAUGHTERS OF MEN

DISCUSSION:

Genesis 6 is one of my favorite yet one of the most misunderstood chapters in the Bible, but after this study, I hope you will have a better grasp of it. As we delve into this passage, I must note that Moses is the author of Genesis. Interestingly, the Genesis events did not occur while Moses was alive. That is pretty peculiar. All the Hebrew scholars, rabbis, and even Jewish traditions say that Moses wrote Genesis. It was given to him on the mountain of God; therefore, the entire book is supernatural. We must understand that he wrote it out as it was dictated to him. With that said, the specific wording, phrases, and order is there for a reason.

- ❖ To understand the origin of spiritual warfare, you must break Genesis 6 down, read every word, and group it into phrases.

- ❖ **Genesis 6:1:**

  Now it came to pass, when men began to multiply on the face of the earth, and daughters were born to them.

  - Genesis 6:1 states that the people on the earth began to multiply, and daughters were born to them.

- The reason it starts this way is not only to describe the process of multiplication among human beings but to set it up for the revelation of what else occurred.

- This passage speaks of daughters born to men, and the following phrase describes different beings.

- The sons of God differ from daughters born from the people on the earth.

- Notice that this verse does not say the sons of God began to multiply on the planet; it says that men or human beings began to multiply on the face of the earth.

- So, the humans and the daughters born to them were one set of entities, and the sons of God were another distinct set.

❖ <u>Genesis 6:2:</u>

That the sons of God saw the daughters of men, that they were beautiful; and they took wives for themselves of all whom they chose.

- The sons of God saw the beautiful women or the daughters of men, and they took any they wanted as their wives.

- The problem was that the sons of God were giant hybrid races, like the ones in later times that Samson dealt with in Judges 14–16.

- The Jewish people, including Samson, were forbidden to marry anyone from other countries (Deuteronomy 7:3; Judges 14:3), especially from the Philistine camps known to have these hybrids.

- This interbreeding problem started during the period before the flood in Genesis and then crept up again afterward.

What was the difference between the sons of God and the daughters of men?

_____
_____
_____
_____
_____

What was the result of the interbreeding between these different beings?

_____
_____
_____
_____
_____

THE SERPENT'S SEED

DISCUSSION:

The devil knew that Jesus had to come through a pure human body, so he attempted to infiltrate humanity to thwart God's plan. If he could cause people to interbreed to where they were no longer fully human but part animal or some other entity, then Jesus couldn't be the perfect sacrifice without blemish. Jesus had to come through a genetically pure human line to redeem us (1 Peter 1:18-19).

The world became so corrupt that Noah and his family of eight were the only pure humans left. Only the eight people on the ark were perfect in their generations or genetically pure (Genesis 6:8–17). They were the only ones who did not allow the serpent's seed to corrupt their bloodlines. God destroyed the rest in the great flood of Noah's time (Genesis 7).

❖ After Adam and Eve fell in the Garden of Eden, satan immediately went after the woman's seed. He tried to intercept God's plan to send our Deliverer, Jesus Christ.

❖ <u>Genesis 3:14–15 AMP:</u>
The Lord God said to the serpent, "Because you have done this, you are cursed more than all the cattle, and more than any animal of the field; On your belly you shall go, and dust you shall eat all the days of your life. And I will put enmity (open hostility) between you and the woman, and between your seed (offspring) and her Seed; He shall [fatally] bruise your head, and you shall [only] bruise. His heel."

- The sons of God were the sons of Adam who lived for 800–900 years periods after the fall.

- The line of Adam's son Cain, who sinned by killing his brother, Abel (Genesis 4), bore the devil's offspring.

- He was the one through which this hybrid line came and where they were infiltrated. Genesis 3:15 prophesied that the offspring of the serpent would bite and bruise the heel of the woman's offspring; this Scripture reveals what happened.

- Cain rebelled against God; Hebrews 11:4 says that his brother, Abel, was righteous, and Cain was not.

- If you study the lineage of Cain, you will see the corruption that infiltrated his genealogy.

- Cain was cursed because he murdered his brother, and his offspring were the seed of the serpent.

- Of course, God never intended for Abel to be killed.

- The bottom line is that the sons of God interbred with the daughters of men, and at a certain point, God intervened.

❖ **Genesis 6:3:**

And the Lord said, "My Spirit shall not strive with man forever, for he is indeed flesh; yet his days shall be one hundred and twenty years."

- God was so upset with the human beings' wickedness that He limited their average lifespan to no more than 120 years (Genesis 6:3–7).

- The Lord did not want interbreeding to take place, nor did He want hybrid offspring to live longer because of how corrupt they were.

- Not everyone was evil at that time, but the situation with humanity was terrible for the most part.

- God's Spirit wouldn't strive with human beings anymore, so He decided to curb their wickedness.

How did the enemy use the seed of the serpent to corrupt humanity?

_____
_____
_____
_____

What was God's response to the wickedness on the earth in Genesis 6?

_____
_____
_____
_____

UNDERSTANDING THE NEPHILIM

DISCUSSION:

As I previously mentioned, we must divide the entities in Genesis 6 into subsets to understand what took place. There are the sons of God, the daughters of men, and the Nephilim. The Nephilim were wicked because they left their abode and taught humans how to sin (Jude 6). They were the fallen angels with lucifer in the Garden of Eden. The root of Nephilim is *napal*, which means *to fall* or be *cast down*[1]. The devil originally was a bright and shiny one, whose name was actually *helel*, according to Isaiah 14:12[2]. You can see that the Hebrew word used there is not lucifer; it's the word *helel*, which means *the bright and shining one of God*.

❖ <u>Genesis 6:4 ESV:</u>

The Nephilim were on the earth in those days, and also afterward, when the sons of God came in to the daughters of man and they bore children to them. These were the mighty men who were of old, the men of renown.

- In addition to the sons of God and the daughters of men, Genesis 6:4 mentions another subset of entities.

- It says in those days and for some time afterward, the Nephilim lived on the earth.

- This verse explains that the sons of God had intercourse with the women who gave birth to children who became the heroes and famous warriors of ancient times.

- The sons of God and daughters of men crossed over the boundary that God set.

❖ <u>Jude 1:6–7 ESV:</u>

And the angels who did not stay within their own position of authority, but left their proper dwelling, He has kept in eternal chains under gloomy darkness until the judgment of the great day—just as Sodom and Gomorrah and the surrounding cities, which likewise indulged in sexual immorality and pursued

---

1 "H5307 - nāpāl - Strong's Hebrew Lexicon (esv)." Blue Letter Bible. Accessed 30 Jun, 2023. https://www.blueletterbible.org/lexicon/h5307/esv/wlc/0-1/
2 "H1966 - hêlēl - Strong's Hebrew Lexicon (kjv)." Blue Letter Bible. Accessed 30 Jun, 2023. https://www.blueletterbible.org/lexicon/h1966/kjv/wlc/0-1/

unnatural desire, serve as an example by undergoing a punishment of eternal fire.

❖ **2 Peter 2:4 ESV:**

For if God did not spare angels when they sinned, but cast them into hell and committed them to chains of gloomy darkness to be kept until the judgment.

- The Nephilim were the fallen angels that left their abode; according to Peter and Jude, they are now in chains.

- Since these fallen angels are chained, they cannot be the demons inhabiting people on earth.

- These angels are the ones who taught people to sin by influencing the sons of God to go into the daughters of men, causing this interbreeding to happen in Genesis 6.

- The Nephilim who left their abode were the ones who influenced people to sin, not the ones who went into the daughters of men.

- The Scripture states that the Nephilim were on the earth in those days, and the sons of God went into the daughters of men.

- Several things are going on here which cannot be interchanged. I wanted to thoroughly explain these verses because this is one of the most misunderstood topics in the Bible.

Who were the Nephilim, and how did they influence the people of the earth?

_____

_____

_____

_____

❖ **Mark 12:25:**

For when they rise from the dead, they neither marry nor are given in marriage, but are like angels in heaven.

- It doesn't surprise me that satan would create confusion about angels, demons, and spiritual warfare because he seeks to deceive and discredit believers.

- Angels cannot procreate. The enemy wants you to believe and speak things that are not true.

- Jesus clearly states in Mark 12:25 that we won't have marriages when we get to Heaven; we will be like the angels.

- The angels don't get married because they don't have a gender. Although they can appear as men or women, they are actually genderless.

- Angels are beings God created. They live beyond this realm and do not procreate.

- Nowhere in the Bible does it say that angels can have children.

- It is impossible for angels to interbreed with human beings; however, they can cloak themselves and appear human.

- Angels have done that with all of us, and most of the time, we don't even know about it.

- To have children, you have to be a human being.

- These truths in Genesis 6 must be taken word for word, phrase by phrase, and put into subsets, as I call them; Mark 11:25 will help you.

❖ <u>1 Peter 1:19:</u>
But with the precious blood of Christ, as of a lamb without blemish and without spot.

- The interbreeding between the sons of God and the daughters of men caused these giant, fierce warriors to be born.

- These giants had genetic defects, which is why the whole idea of a spotless lamb matters.

- Spotless and without blemish meant that there were no genetic defects.

- The genetic defects came because of interbreeding.

- You can see defects in animals and humans today, but this was never God's will.

To summarize, a whole race on the earth had interbred before the flood; they were all hybrids except for Noah's family. Remember that there were only eight who made it onto the ark. Out of millions of people on the earth, only eight were pure. God used their pure genealogy to preserve the lineage of the Messiah through the flood.

HYBRID BEINGS AFTER THE FLOOD

DISCUSSION:

We see the giant races pop up again because genetic material was brought across the flood, which again infiltrated the human race. This infiltration is addressed through Noah, who said, "Cursed be Canaan" (Genesis 9:24-25); there's your clue. Genetic corruption occurred before and after the flood; the giant races returned. Joshua and David were used as mighty warriors to defeat the giant races (Numbers 13:28-33; Joshua 11:21-23; 1 Samuel 17:50-53). When Israel entered the promised land and started to inhabit it, they drove out all these races and eventually extinguished the hybrid giants.

- ❖ **Genesis 10:8-10 ESV:**

    Cush fathered Nimrod; he was the first on earth to be a mighty man. He was a mighty hunter before the Lord. Therefore it is said, "Like Nimrod a mighty hunter before the Lord." The beginning of his kingdom was Babel, Erech, Accad, and Calneh, in the land of Shinar.

    - Genesis 10:8 says that Nimrod was a mighty one who was one of the hybrids.

    - Before the flood, hybrid beings were able to build the pyramids and other structures that we can't even construct today.

    - After the flood, Nimrod began to restart that by building the Tower of Babel, so God had to come down and stop him (Genesis 11:1-9).

    - Nimrod, who was known as the first architect, was deified and became known as Gilgamesh.

- That is where the mystical Mystery Babylon, in Revelation 17, originated from.

❖ In Greek mythology, there are many so-called gods, which you may have seen portrayed in paintings. I have investigated some of the art from the walls of Babylon that Nimrod built and have reason to believe that hybrids may have inspired these images.

DISEMBODIED SPIRITS

DISCUSSION:

Spiritual warfare started in the Garden of Eden with helel deceiving Adam and Eve, causing their eyes to be opened to good and evil so that he could have his way with them (Genesis 3:1-7). Once he deceived them and they ate, they knew the difference between good and evil. Human beings did not previously know evil because it was something that only God could handle. After they ate the fruit, they were cursed and driven out of the garden (Genesis 3:17-24). Instead of living forever, they now had a limited lifespan. People then started fighting disease, sin, and the results of the fall of man, leading us to where we are today.

In the Old Testament, we mostly read about wars in the flesh; there were many battles between the people of God and those giant hybrid races. Joshua, David, and others dealt with them through natural warfare. We don't see a lot of demonic activity until David appears. When observing David's life, you can see a parallel between the natural and spiritual realms. At one point, satan rose up against David and tempted him to sin by counting his fighting men (1 Chronicles 21:1-8). It was forbidden in the law to have confidence in your fighting armies. So when he ordered them to be counted, satan was actually fighting against Israel. We start to see in that passage that the natural realm is influenced by the unseen demonic realm.

- ❖ Genesis 6:5–7 ESV:

    The Lord saw that the wickedness of man was great in the earth, and that every intention of the thoughts of his was only evil continually. And the Lord regretted that he had made man on the earth, and it grieved him to his heart. So the Lord said, "I will blot out man whom I have created from the face of the land, man and animals and creeping things and birds of the heavens, for I am sorry that I have made them."

    - The Lord saw that the wickedness on the earth was so evil that He destroyed all the human hybrids and animals in the flood except for the ones that He chose to be on the ark.

    - God's heart was grieved, and He was sorry that He had made man and put them on the earth.

    - The Lord decided to wipe out the human race that He created from the face of the planet.

    - The bodies of these people were destroyed, which caused their spirits to become disembodied. These are now the demons that we deal with on the earth today.

    - Not only did God destroy the people, but also large and small animals, and even birds. He actually said, "I'm sorry that I ever made them."

    - Only Noah found favor in the sight of the Lord because he had kept himself and his family pure (Genesis 6:8–9).

❖ <u>Mark 1:23–26:</u>
Now there was a man in their synagogue with an unclean spirit. And he cried out, saying, "Let us alone! What have we to do with You, Jesus of Nazareth? Did You come to destroy us? I know who You are—the Holy One of God!" But Jesus rebuked him, saying, "Be quiet, and come out of him!" And when the unclean spirit had convulsed him and cried out with a loud voice, he came of out him.

- As mentioned, we can see in the Bible that the fallen angels are all chained.

- Notice that when Jesus was addressing demons, He wasn't addressing fallen angels but unclean spirits.

- Notably, these were perverse or unclean spirits—the rebellious spirits of the hybrid people who lived before the flood.

- Demons are disembodied spirits. That's why they seek embodiment because they once had a body.

Where did demons come from, and why do they seek embodiment?

_____
_____
_____
_____
_____

How has satan gained access to humans from Adam and Eve throughout human history?

_____

_____

_____

_____

_____

CHAPTER 2

THE ENEMY'S COVERT OPERATION

Put on the whole armor of God, that you may be able to stand against the wiles of the devil.
—Ephesians 6:11

DISCUSSION:

In the previous chapter, we discussed how demons came to be. As mentioned, the demonic realm wasn't revealed in the Bible until the time of King David. When we study David's life, we will see how spiritual warfare directly influenced his natural battles. After Goliath was killed, his spirit was disembodied because that's what happened with the hybrid beings. Today, we are still warring with these disembodied spirits.

David faced many struggles throughout his life and was essentially driven into sin. His trials were the workings of demonic spirits which fought against him. People in the Old Testament didn't have the help we have today. They didn't have the name of Jesus, spiritual gifts, or the Holy Spirit inside them.

❖ <u>Isaiah 10:27 KJV:</u>

And it shall come to pass in that day, that his burden shall be taken away from off thy shoulder, and his yoke from off thy neck, and the yoke shall be destroyed because of the anointing.

- In the Old Testament, God's people had prophets, priests, and kings who had the Holy Spirit upon them but not within them.

- As New Testament believers, we now have the anointing both upon and within us (John 14:16-17).

- That which is within us is much more powerful than that which is upon us.

- However, when it comes to the anointing, it breaks the yoke, so we'll take all we can get.

As New Testament believers, what help do we have that the Old Testament believers did not have? What does the anointing do for us?

_____
_____
_____
_____
_____

PARALLEL REALMS

DISCUSSION:

In some Old Testament accounts, prophets reveal what happened behind the scenes in the unseen realm. For example, Ezekiel addresses both the natural and spiritual rulers of Tyre. In Ezekiel 28:1-10, he confronted a man; then you see a shift in verses 11-18 where he exposed the fallen covering cherub in the Garden of Eden—satan himself. Similarly, Isaiah prophesied against Babylon's prideful, earthly king in Isaiah 14:3-11. Then, in verses 12-17, he pronounced the judgment of helel, who lifted himself up against God in pride. Again, we see satan behind the scenes. These are just two examples of how the parallel realms operate together.

Even though we have a glimpse of spiritual warfare through the Old Testament prophets, Paul addressed this subject in more detail throughout the New Testament. He explains the armor that God has given us to stand against the demonic realm in Ephesians 6 and 2 Corinthians 10. Interestingly, he doesn't talk much about the entities themselves but focuses more on instructing believers on executing their authority and gaining victory over them.

❖ <u>Ephesians 6:10–17 AMP:</u>

In conclusion, be strong in the Lord [draw your strength from Him and be empowered through the union with Him] and in the power of his [boundless] might. Put on the full armor of God [for his precepts are like the splendid armor of a heavily-armed soldier], so that you may be able to [successfully] stand up against all the schemes and the strategies and the deceits of the devil. For our struggle is not against flesh and blood [contending only with physical opponents], but against the rulers, against the powers, against the world forces of this [present] darkness, against the spiritual forces of wickedness in the heavenly (supernatural) places. Therefore, put on the complete armor of God, so that you will be able to [successfully] resist and stand your ground in the day of evil [of danger], and having done everything [that the crisis demands], to stand firm [in your place, fully prepared, immovable, victorious]. So stand firm and hold your ground, having tightened the wide band of truth (personal integrity, moral courage) around your waist and having put on the breastplate of righteousness (an upright heart), and having strapped on your feet the gospel of peace in preparation [to face the enemy with firm-footed stability and readiness produced by good news]. Above all, lift up the protective shield of faith with which you can extinguish all the flaming arrows of the evil one. And take the helmet of salvation, and the sword of the Spirit, which is the Word of God.

- Ephesians 6, the most descriptive chapter in the Bible for spiritual warfare, explains the armor of God.

- Notice how this chapter is worded; we are actually defending the faith. We are not obtaining anything because we already have all that we need.

- Paul charged believers to make a stand in every situation as though they already own and occupy territory in the kingdom of God.

- With this armor, we are instructed to stand guard and defend what we have been given through Christ.

- Notice that most of the pieces of armor are defensive, not offensive.

- The only offensive weapon is the sword of the Spirit, which is the Word of God. This sword should be used aggressively against the enemy.

- We must understand our armor.

- Paul mentions four different sectors of opponents that war against people which are not flesh and blood; in other words, they are not human beings.

What are we instructed to do with the armor given to us in Ephesians 6:10-17?

_____

_____

_____

_____

DISCUSSION:

Notice that in the Old Testament, everybody went to war against each other. As we discussed, there was no discernment about evil spirits until David came along. The first mention of an evil spirit in the Bible is the one that Saul dealt with, which is significant (1 Samuel 16:14–23). When that spirit would come and harass him, David played the harp, and it would leave.

There is no mention of demons before the one that distressed Saul. As previously mentioned, disembodied spirits were there from the hybrids who perished in the flood. In the Hebrew language, they are not labeled as angels. Different words are used for angels, which are not used in 1 Samuel 16. The Bible is distinct in the description of evil spirits versus angels.

The New Testament is where we get some detail about spiritual warfare. Amazingly, Paul said we are not wrestling against physical opponents, which is what they did in the Old Testament. They were constantly fighting because the hybrids were alive. Post-flood, God's people still warred with those half-breeds, which was what God wanted them to do; however, remember by that time that behind the scenes, millions of disembodied, evil spirits were also among them. So it was quite a struggle.

What is the difference between warfare described in the Old and New Testaments?

_____

_____

_____

_____

DEMONIC DIVISIONS

DISCUSSION:

Today, we are contending against rulers, powers, world forces of this present darkness, and spiritual forces of wickedness in the heavenly, supernatural places. So, Ephesians 6:12 mentions four different divisions. Even though Paul does not go into much detail, they are all significant. Perhaps he personally expounded on the topic with congregations like the church in Ephesus; maybe he assumed they were already familiar with these divisions. I want to find more material on the people from that time. Would it not be nice to have the notes of those who attended Paul's meetings? All we know from Scripture is that there are these four divisions, which are all important.

Even after significant study, it is still unclear what these beings in Ephesians 6 really are. Yet I can tell you that I have encountered different species and levels in spiritual warfare. You have, too. There has been quite a bit of confusion because it's not like what has been taught and depicted, such as the image of the red devil with horns and a pitchfork.

Only once have I seen a creature with horns: a very tall hideous giant being that stood upright and appeared to be half human and half goat. Somebody walked into our house in Seattle, so I went upstairs, and there it was, at least eight or nine feet tall. It would have had to stoop to get through the door if it even used doors. He was just standing there. When I researched it later, I saw a picture of baal. That's who it was; I cannot even describe the hideousness.

If you do a study on baal, you can see that the covert image of this figure appears in many events today, such as commercials and satanic rituals on TV before ball games. You can look it up on the internet and see that same being. I don't recommend staring at these images, but we are seeing them more publicly. They even appear on T-shirts and in different stores. I believe that this baal creature that appeared in my house was lucifer.

❖ **Jeremiah 19:5:**
They have also built the high places of baal, to burn their sons with fire for burnt offerings to baal, which I did not command or speak, nor did it come into My mind.

- In the Old Testament, children were sacrificed to baal on altars.

- If you research what is happening in our culture and world, you can see that children are still being sacrificed to baal in various ways.

- I now understand that baal is actually satan. He is just one being.

- I have seen other types of evil entities parading themselves in different ways.

- Some demonic entities look like angels, whereas others look like creatures from another planet, but they're not. These are demons from a specific hierarchy.

- Demonic entities have many different forms, including those that look like lizards and furry animals.

❖ We mainly deal with the earthbound demons, which are the ones that we were given authority over through Christ.

❖ Luke 10:19 says we have authority over serpents and scorpions, which are symbolic of demons who walk or crawl along the ground.

❖ Jesus essentially came as a human being and dealt with those entities that human beings have authority over, which are disembodied spirits.

Which entities have we been given authority over, according to Luke 10:19?

_____

_____

_____

_____

_____

❖ Zechariah 10:2:

For the idols speak delusion; The diviners envision lies, and tell false dreams; They comfort in vain. Therefore the people wend their way like sheep; They are in trouble because there is no shepherd.

- The Bible mentions different heavenly beings, such as seraphim and cherubim (Isaiah 6:1-3; Ezekiel 10:14-15).

- We have already discussed the Nephilim, which are fallen angels who are now chained.

- There are also *teraphim*[3]. This word is derived from *terra*, which means earthbound.

- In several Scriptures, teraphim are mentioned as idols, such as the household gods Jacob's wife, Rachel, stole from her father, Laban (Genesis 31:19).

- However, if we dive a little deeper, the Bible reveals that they are those disembodied, earthbound demons that masquerade themselves.

- For example, Zechariah 10:2 describes the idols as speaking delusion. It was not the wood and stone talking but the disembodied spirits hiding behind them.

- These covert demons used deception to gain access and occupy people, aiming to infiltrate genetics.

INFILTRATION OF HUMAN DNA

DISCUSSION:

If you research, you find that the enemy is still seeking to alter human DNA, just like in the days of Noah; it's happening again. One way to get into the DNA and change people's genetics is through the liver. This corruption has occurred through disease-causing bacteria which mutate in the human body. There is classified information showing certain strains of bacteria, which are living organisms, that can cause a conversion in the human liver. So that's what these entities use to work their way into your DNA.

---

3 "H8655 - tᵊrāpîm - Strong's Hebrew Lexicon (kjv)." Blue Letter Bible. Accessed 9 Jul, 2023. https://www.blueletterbible.org/lexicon/h8655/kjv/wlc/0-1/

If you want to know how the serpent infiltrated the blood of a human being, you can research mutations that came from bacteria affecting the liver. However, you must be careful when doing this type of research because you will be tracked. You can observe that the Bible gives many clues about the covert strategies of the enemy that are hidden behind the scenes. If you study the liver and the impact of these bacteria on human beings, you will see how this infiltration takes place. DNA-altering bacteria are not of God; they are microscopic demonic entities. God did not create bacteria to be rogue and harmful, yet they can be carriers that can penetrate the human DNA and cause conversion. These truths are hidden from the masses.

The hierarchy of demonic forces, mentioned in Ephesians 6, aims to infiltrate and influence the human race. As such, satan wants to accelerate this so that he can obtain the human race as fast as possible. The enemy would have prevailed if God had not slowed everything down. He destroyed the earth once, kept eight pure people, and restarted the world. Even afterward, these genetically altered hybrids appeared again. God then raised up David, Samson, and others to kill off all these giant races.

- ❖ In the Old Testament, God's people were forbidden to interbreed with certain races because they had hybrid DNA. The Israelites were separated as a people because God wanted a pure stock human race so that when Jesus came in the flesh, He would come as a pure human being.

- ❖ **Hebrews 10:12 NLT:**

    But our High Priest offered Himself to God as a single sacrifice for sins, good for all time. Then He sat down in the place of honor at God's right hand.

    - Jesus was the perfect sacrifice.

- If Jesus had any kind of altered DNA in His blood that was hybrid or from the serpent's seed, He would not have been able to redeem us.

- You can see that although satan tried to prevent it from happening, God preserved the human race.

- Jesus came through Mary, a pure human being.

- All the genealogies show that Mary's lines didn't interbreed with these races of people on the earth at different times.

- Jesus was the pure and spotless Lamb (John 1:29)—without blemish, genetic defect, or any reptilian blood in Him.

Why were the Israelites forbidden to intermarry with certain races in the Old Testament?

_____
_____
_____
_____
_____

How is satan still attempting to corrupt human DNA today?

_____
_____
_____
_____
_____

STAY WITHIN GOD'S BOUNDARIES

DISCUSSION:

In spiritual warfare, we are dealing with the four levels of entities that Paul mentioned. We are called to resist and obtain dominion over them through the truth that Jesus already defeated them. However, it does say that individually, we have power over all the enemy, but Luke 10:19 states that we are to trample on serpents and scorpions, which are the earthbound ones that crawl along the ground. It doesn't mention trampling on the other entities, so we must stay within our parameters.

Some individuals presumptuously confronted entities by themselves, but God never gave them authority to deal with those entities. These people were killed. Intercessors have prayed against demonic powers in the heavenly realms, which unfortunately cost them their lives. Previously, I didn't understand why I was losing so many good people in my life. They were bold and came against these entities in high places outside the Holy Spirit's leading.

Clearly, Jesus only dealt with the unclean spirits and earthbound demons from the hybrid races. When Jesus was on the earth, He drove demons out of people; He did not directly expel principalities or powers from their position in the atmosphere. He said He saw satan fall like lightning, but He does not even mention any of these other levels that Paul does. We do not know much about these different entities; therefore, it is wise for us to stay within the boundaries of authority that the Lord has given us through His Word.

Why must we stay within God's set boundaries concerning spiritual warfare?

_____
_____
_____
_____
_____

CHAPTER 3

Parameters of Spiritual Authority

So Jesus said, "I speak to you eternal truth. The Son is unable to do anything from Himself or through His own initiative. I only do the works that I see the Father doing, for the Son does the same works as His Father."
—John 5:19 TPT

DISCUSSION:

The groundwork for deliverance has been established in our first two chapters. We discussed how Jesus only dealt with demons inhabiting people; He did not address those that were not in people. By now, we understand that entities are everywhere that do not dwell in people. Paul lists this hierarchy in Ephesians 6. However, Jesus did not directly deal with those. He delivered people from earthbound, disembodied spirits, the same demons that we are charged to trample.

In the future, Jesus, the saints, and angels will come, wage war, and conquer the enemy's army. That is for a time that is coming. As mentioned, I've lost some friends who presumptuously engaged these entities in spiritual warfare. Over the following several years, I investigated this and uncovered more information. When my research was complete, I had exhausted mysterious subjects, including UFOs and dinosaurs. My initial research process generated more questions; towards the end, especially concerning UFOs, I came to unquestionable conclusions. I finally just took all my work and destroyed it.

Too much detail about these subjects will cause division and confusion because people are not ready; I was not even prepared for what I found out. Maybe you are, but I must be wise concerning the information I release because I learned that world governments are involved. Therefore, there is no reason to address something the Bible does not discuss.

- ❖ Jesus defeated all of the enemy's army on the cross. However, the ultimate enforcement of this victory over these other entities will take place at the end of the age, when they are all thrown into the lake of fire (Revelation 20:7–10).
- ❖ Through my research, I realized that those levels of entities we are dealing with have to do with the coming end-time deception.

What will satan use to cause end-time deception? When will the ultimate defeat of these spiritual enemies be carried out?

_____
_____
_____
_____
_____

TERRITORIAL SPIRITS IN THE AIR

❖ **Revelation 17:13-14 AMP:**

These [kings] have one purpose [one mind, one common goal], and they give their power and authority to the beast. They will wage war against the Lamb (Christ), and the Lamb will triumph and conquer them, because He is Lord of lords and King of kings, and those who are with Him and on His side are the called and chosen (elect) and faithful.

- Demonic influence has infiltrated governments.

- When you start to understand and communicate what is happening with these entities we have been discussing, you will also find yourself dealing with authorities in the flesh.

- The Lord has not called me to do that. I'm called to preach the gospel and minister deliverance as part of the package.

Read Revelation 17:13-14. What must we understand about the spirit and natural realms working together in governments? What should we focus on?

_____
_____
_____
_____
_____

❖ **Jude 1:8–9 NLT:**

In the same way, these people—who claim authority from their dreams—live immoral lives, defy authority, and scoff at supernatural beings. But even Michael, one of the mightiest of the angels, did not dare accuse the devil of blasphemy, but simply said, "The Lord rebuke you!" (This took place when Michael was arguing with the devil about Moses' body.)

- It is imperative that we stay within God's set boundaries when dealing with spiritual warfare.

- Do not be presumptuous.

- Each one of us needs help in fighting against these evil spirits.

- The various entities in the higher places are not part of the earthbound demons we have been given the authority to deal with directly.

- The corporate anointing upon a congregation of believers can come against these spirits when the Lord permits them.

- When the body of Christ comes together, there is greater power in agreement because of the numbers. So at times, we can confront these spirits as a body.

- Individually, we have been given authority over serpents, scorpions, and all the enemy's power—the evil spirits on the earth.

- The book of Revelation speaks of demonic rulers influencing our world leaders—those who are at a high level and can control countries (Revelation 17).

- The church of the Lord Jesus Christ could agree and push back these entities; however, it is not wise for individuals to attempt this.

In Jude 1:8-9, how did the archangel, Michael, respond to the devil?

_____
_____
_____
_____

What is the difference between our spiritual authority as individuals compared to the corporate body of Christ?

_____
_____
_____
_____

- <u>Mark 5:8-13 NLT</u>

   For Jesus had already said to the spirit, "Come out the man, you evil spirit." Then Jesus demanded, "What is your name?" And he replied, "My name is Legion, because there are many of us inside this man." Then the evil spirits begged him again and again not to send them to some distant place. There happened to be a large herd of pigs feeding on the hillside nearby. "Send us into those pigs," the spirits begged. "Let us enter them." So Jesus gave them permission. The evil spirits came out of the man and entered the pigs, and the entire herd of about 2,000 pigs plunged down the steep hillside into the lake and drowned in the water.

❖ <u>Mark 5:20 NLT</u>

So the man started off to visit the Ten Towns of that region and began to proclaim the great things Jesus had done for him; and everyone was amazed at what he told them.

- People may encounter higher-level entities that don't necessarily inhabit people but control the lower-level disembodied spirits in a particular area who do.

- There are territorial strongholds in cities and regions, so you may sometimes bump into more than just the spirits you drive out of people.

- Jesus faced this situation when He was driving out demons and encountered legion (Mark 5:1–20; Luke 8:26–39).

- I believe that legion was the entity that was a stronghold over that city and territory.

- You may encounter something similar.

Why do demonic spirits want to remain in their prospective territories?

_____

_____

_____

_____

_____

DISCUSSION:

Ruling spirits, the powers dominating the nations, have performed feats that people cannot do today. The pyramids and mysterious marks on the earth were accomplished with help from entities in high places. From the air, you can see tattoos on the planet. There were no airplanes at the time when they were created, yet people somehow had the ability to be in the air.

Why would someone create designs that point directly towards true or magnetic north when viewed from the air? These wouldn't be needed unless you were in the air. Something was happening that had been hidden from us. I believe that governments have hidden these findings from the public because satan, the prince of the power of the air, wants to keep his tactics covert.

BE PREPARED FOR RESISTANCE

DISCUSSION:

If you're sent somewhere on an assignment, the idea in Ephesians 6:10-18 is that you're dressed for it. You are prepared to defend what God has sent you to do. You are on a mission and will accomplish it, yet you will face resistance during that mission. That's the whole concept of spiritual warfare; it's what Jesus did throughout His earthly ministry.

- ❖ Jesus did not seek to uproot the devil or pull down strongholds from the air. He cast ground-level demons out of people and never even addressed the higher-ups.

- ❖ **James 4:7:**

  Therefore submit to God. Resist the devil and he will flee from you.

- ❖ **1 Corinthians 15:57–58:**

  But thanks be to God, who gives us the victory through our Lord Jesus Christ. Therefore, my beloved brethren, be steadfast, immovable, always abounding in the work of the Lord, knowing that your labor is not in vain in the Lord.

  - We are given authority to deal with earthbound demons in people and are instructed to resist them, standing our ground in the evil day.

  - According to 1 Corinthians 15:57–58, we must remain immovable, stay in our place, and be victorious, tightening everything up and holding our ground.

  - Ephesians 6 gives us all of the different pieces of protective armor.

  - It doesn't tell us to be aggressive but just to stand firm.

- ❖ **Matthew 8:16 AMP:**

  When evening came, they brought to Him many who were under the power of demons; and He cast out the evil spirits with a word, and restored to health all who were sick [exhibiting His authority as Messiah].

  - It's worth mentioning again that I do not go after these territorial spirits.

- Jesus didn't go out and look for demons; they came at Him when He arrived in different places (Mark 5:2).
- He wasn't looking for them and didn't call them out.
- I know this is a paradigm shift for many people, but scripture clearly says this.
- I'm not looking for a battle or spiritual warfare. I'm not seeking it; however, it will come because I'm sent.

How did Jesus deal with demonic spirits?

_____
_____
_____
_____
_____

According to James 4:7 and 1 Corinthians 15:57–58, how should we wage spiritual warfare?

_____
_____
_____
_____
_____

FOCUS ON GOD'S ASSIGNMENT

DISCUSSION:

When Jesus spoke with governmental authorities, such as Pilate and Herod, He never addressed the entities behind them (Luke 23:6–25). But wherever Jesus went, if a demon needed to be dealt with at the time, it manifested, and He drove it out. So, think about the fact that Jesus never addressed territorial spirits that influenced world leaders. He was just out and about in the countryside or the synagogue, and these demon spirits would start manifesting. Jesus just preached the gospel; this is what we're supposed to do. I want to straighten this out and simplify it for you because it can be easy.

I do not go out looking for aliens, Big Foot, or different hierarchies of evil spirits. Jesus defeated every wicked entity on the cross, but He told us to cast out demons, which are essentially in people. Let's be honest: How many people do you think have the spiritual sensitivity to know that a demon is in someone without it talking or manifesting? The bottom line is that most of the time, we know because they start to get fidgety. They begin speaking through the person and manifesting, which is what happened with Jesus.

Jesus wasn't looking for a fight. He was sent places to preach the gospel, and the demons got in the way, so they were driven out. In Ephesians 6 you find the first stage of the hierarchy, which can be dealt with on an individual level. The other three groups should be dealt with through the corporate body. Congregations of believers can displace territorial entities in their area when a strong presence of God is dwelling in their midst. You really have to be Spirit-led to take out these higher echelons, and it has to be done through the body of Christ.

- ❖ It is always best to stay within your parameters and understand that you are wearing protective armor. The sword of the Spirit is the only offensive weapon; the rest of your armor is defensive.

- ❖ We are called to stand and defend the faith. In doing so, demons will find you; you don't need to seek them out. That is just the way it is. It is how Jesus dealt with the enemy, so that's how we should deal with it.

What are we called to do? How do demons respond when we fulfill our calling?

_____
_____
_____
_____
_____

ALWAYS PRAY IN THE SPIRIT

DISCUSSION:

True warfare is being completely dressed in the defensive armor and praying in the Spirit at all times with all types of prayer in every season. We must maintain this stance, stay alert, and persevere in prayer for all of God's people.

Paul asked the Ephesians to pray for him. His thought process behind this request is that because he was in chains, he wanted boldness to open his mouth and proclaim the mystery of the good news of salvation. He described himself as an "ambassador in chains." He was in jail, which was a result of spiritual warfare. As Paul said, we are supposed to be praying.

❖ **Ephesians 6:18–20 AMP:**

With all prayer and petition pray [with specific requests] at all times [on every occasion and in every season] in the Spirit, and with this in view, stay alert with all perseverance and petition [interceding in prayer] for all God's people. And pray for me, that words may be given to me when I open my mouth, to proclaim boldly the mystery of the good news [of salvation], for which I am an ambassador in chains. And pray that in proclaiming it I may speak boldly and courageously, as I should.

- After listing all of the armor in Ephesians 6, verse 18 instructs us to pray in the Spirit all the time, everywhere we go.

- With this in mind, we must stay alert and persevere in intercession for God's people.

- Paul asked for prayer for the words and boldness to proclaim the gospel. He explained that he was an ambassador in chains.

- Guess who put him in chains? It was the devil.

- In his letter, Paul gave the Ephesians all the information he could share about spiritual warfare, and then he essentially said, "Now pray."

How are we supposed to pray, according to Ephesians 6:18–20?

_____

_____

_____

_____

_____

❖ Daniel 2:42–43 AMP:

As the [ten] toes of the feet were partly of iron and partly of clay, so some of the kingdom will be strong, and another part of it will be brittle. And as you saw the iron mixed with common clay, so they will combine with one another in the seed of men; but they will not merge [for such diverse things or ideologies cannot unite], even as iron does not mix with clay.

- As the body of Christ prays, these entities that claim to be from another planet but are really from another realm will be exposed.

- They are not from another planet but from another realm; they are part of the evil echelons of satan.

- Ultimately, they will try to intertwine themselves with the human race.

- Daniel 2 alludes to this in describing the image of the statue, made of different substances from the head down to the ten toes. Those of the kingdom mentioned in verses 42–43 tried to mix with the seed of men, but it would not take, just like clay cannot mix with iron.

- You may be thinking _it's unclear who "they" refers to in this passage_, but I'm telling you who they are.

- Daniel saw that some kind of mixture would happen with the human race at the end of days, symbolized by the ten toes of iron and clay.

- Daniel 2:43 says, "They will combine with one another in the seed of men, but they will not merge."

❖ **Matthew 24:37 AMP:**

For the coming of the Son of Man (the Messiah) will be just like the days of Noah.

- Jesus warned us that before His coming in the end, it will be like it was in the days of Noah (Matthew 24:37–39).

- As I mentioned, there are ways to alter human DNA today, the same way the people were hybridized in Noah's day.

- There is a way to do it through the liver via bacteria; certain diseases and viruses are created as messengers that alter genetics.

- You must be very careful. The bottom line is that your immune system needs to be boosted to keep yourself pure so you don't get infiltrated.

- All kinds of chemicals and substances are processed in our foods. Multiple environmental factors are coming against our immune system.

- Our adversary, satan, wants to break down our natural defenses so that even common viruses that we would typically be able to fight off could enter our genetics through our weakened immune system.

- Spiritually, you must be aware of this; physically, you need to keep your immune system strong.

Why is it essential that we keep our immune systems strong?

_____

_____

_____

_____

_____

REVELATION COMES WITH MATURITY

DISCUSSION:

All believers are given the authority to drive out demons that Jesus defeated. We, the body of Christ, are called to resist the enemy and take our stand so that the gospel can be proclaimed, just like Paul said. This is the background of spiritual warfare. I want to mention that even though there isn't much written in the New Testament about spiritual warfare, as you would think, there is a reason for the apparent information deficit. I believe it is hidden for the same reason Jesus spoke to the masses in parables. As I have, you need to dig for revelation by studying the Scriptures. I discovered hidden truths in God's Word that revealed some nuggets that were not apparent on the surface.

❖ Matthew 13:10–11:

And the disciples came and said to Him, "Why do You speak to them in parables?" He answered and said to them, "Because it has been given to you to know the mysteries of the kingdom of heaven, but to them it has not been given."

- Jesus explained the mysteries of the parables to the disciples so they would eventually be able to share them with the world once they understood.

- One moment, they didn't get the message of the parables; then after Jesus spoke with them, their eyes were opened. He said it was given to them to know the mysteries but not to the masses.

- Why did Jesus teach that way? I believe it's because certain people are not mature enough and wouldn't be able to use this information correctly. It wouldn't be advantageous for them or God.

- Some people are just not ready. We must accept that there are certain mysteries that God has not given to everyone.

DISCUSSION:

If you seek God and show maturity, He will reveal what you are ready for. That is why I'm cautious; I don't feel I'm supposed to share everything God has revealed. If you ask God, He will show you the answers in time. I have been studying some subjects for 20-25 years. I researched a topic for three years; once I found out the truth, I destroyed everything. I had all the evidence you would need to win a case, including photos and letters. However, I realized this information is being hidden for a reason; people aren't ready for it. The coming deception has to do with the end-time scenario; however, it doesn't involve the body of Christ. God's remnant will not be deceived; they will be in the know.

Why does God reveal certain truths to some and not others?

CHAPTER 4

THE BATTLE FOR YOUR MIND

And do not be conformed to this world, but be transformed by the renewing of your mind, that you may prove what is that good and acceptable and perfect will of God.
—Romans 12:2

DISCUSSION:

We have explored some great Scriptures in the previous chapters, revealing what has been happening behind the scenes throughout history. Before diving into the actual process of deliverance, we will uncover the enemy's mode of operation. It is essential to understand his strategies.

You do not always need to know which specific type of entity you're dealing with. Just know, as it has been emphasized, that there are certain spirits that you should not endeavor to confront, such as territorial spirits over your city or state, unless it's in a corporate setting. In Ephesians 6, after Paul described the different spiritual echelons and our protective armor, he concluded that we are to stand firm and pray on all occasions with all kinds of prayer.

❖ <u>Luke 19:10:</u>

For the Son of Man has come to seek and to save that which was lost.

- Remember, Jesus did not pick a fight with the devil.
- The demons manifested as He was doing God's will.

- Despite what deliverance ministries have taught, we should not chase demons.

- During His earthly ministry, Jesus was seeking those who were lost. He wanted people to be saved, healed, and delivered.

- He wasn't doing spiritual warfare by picking a fight.

- Jesus did the will of the Father, and along the way, He encountered demonic resistance.

According to Luke 19:10, what was Jesus's focus?

_____

_____

_____

_____

WAGING WAR IN THE SPIRIT

DISCUSSION:

Paul specifically wrote the way he did for a reason. I encourage you to study his epistles to understand the essence of what he was communicating. He had an indescribable encounter with God when he was caught up in paradise, and thankfully, we are able to glean from what he was permitted to share. There were many things that he was not allowed to share (2 Corinthians 12:4). Likewise, the Lord showed me revelations that I am forbidden to share, some of which have to do with spiritual warfare; however, I reveal what the Lord permits.

Second Corinthians 10 sounds similar to what Paul said in Ephesians 6. He explains that we are not using physical weapons of flesh and blood and reveals our spiritual warfare —destroying any argument that sets itself up above the knowledge of God. We wage war by taking every thought captive, which originates from the soul realm, and subjecting them to the obedience of Christ. This passage builds upon everything we have been discussing in the previous chapters.

❖ **2 Corinthians 10:3–6 AMP:**

For though we walk in the flesh [as mortal men], we are not carrying on our [spiritual] warfare according to the flesh and using the weapons of man. The weapons of our warfare are not physical [weapons of flesh and blood]. Our weapons are divinely powerful for the destruction of fortresses. We are destroying sophisticated arguments and every exalted and proud thing that sets itself up against the [true] knowledge of God, and we are taking every thought and purpose captive to the obedience of Christ, being ready to punish every act of disobedience, when your own obedience [as a church] is complete.

- Spiritual weapons have been given to us, which can be used to dismantle fortresses or strongholds.

- 2 Corinthians 10:3–6 instructs us to tear down every proud argument that sets itself up above the knowledge of God, which is the revelation that has already been given to us through the gospel.

- We must take every thought captive and make them obedient to Christ; that's our warfare.

- It is our responsibility. God will not take our thoughts captive; we need to do that.

- The disobedience of wicked spirits is punished when our obedience as a church is complete.

According to 2 Corinthians 10:3–6, what is our warfare and responsibility?

_____

_____

_____

_____

_____

❖ <u>1 Timothy 4:1-2:</u>

Now the Spirit expressly says that in latter times some will depart from the faith, giving heed to deceiving spirits and doctrines of demons, speaking lies in hypocrisy, having their own conscience seared with a hot iron.

- The Bible reveals that the higher-level echelons will not ultimately reap destruction until the end.

- But now what we are instructed to do is to bring correction.

- Throughout the New Testament, Paul constantly corrected false doctrine and wrong perceptions. Through his teaching, he brought people back into God's way.

- Paul warned Timothy that there would be all kinds of false doctrine in the last days.

- People will be self-seeking and lovers of themselves; some will be so wicked and evil that they will even sell out their parents (2 Timothy 3:1–5).

- We already see a high level of wickedness and deception taking place.

- Paul's letters have been preparing the body of Christ for our last days, which are perilous times, full of all wickedness.

What does Paul warn us will happen in the last days? What did he do through his teachings?

_____

_____

_____

_____

_____

THOUGHTS ARE A GATEWAY

DISCUSSION:

The demonic realm gains entry into the human race through the thought process. Before the fall, Adam and Eve were impenetrable. The enemy could only gain access by deceiving them, causing them to accept a lie. That was difficult to do, mainly because they were hedged in, just like Job, and satan couldn't get to them. He had to be cunning and crafty to infiltrate their minds.

Before Noah's flood, satan's crafty efforts of infiltrating the human race seemed to succeed for a moment. As we discussed, he thought he could stop the Messiah from coming in a human body because he had corrupted the genetics. We discussed the material that altered the DNA; a reptilian type of blood, the serpent's seed, could get into human beings through disease or viruses processed in the liver. God intervened by destroying the world and starting fresh with the eight people He preserved. The disembodied hybrid spirits are now wandering the earth, still seeking to infiltrate the human race.

❖ **Genesis 3:1:**

Now the serpent was more cunning than any beast of the field which the Lord God had made. And he said to the woman, "Has God indeed said, 'You shall not eat of every tree of the garden'?"

❖ **Isaiah 14:12–14:**

How you are fallen from heaven, O lucifer, son of the morning! How you are cut down to the ground, You who weakened the nations! For you have said in your heart: "I will ascend into heaven, I will exalt my throne above the stars of God; I will also sit on the mount of the congregation on the farthest sides of the north; I will ascend above the heights of the clouds, I will be like the Most High."

- How did the devious serpent end up with Adam and Eve in the Garden of Eden? In Genesis 3:1, the Hebrew word for serpent is *nahash*[4], which also can mean *enlightened one*[5].

---

4   "H5175 - nāḥāš - Strong's Hebrew Lexicon (kjv)." Blue Letter Bible. Accessed 12 Jul, 2023. https://www.blueletterbible.org/lexicon/h5175/kjv/wlc/0-1/
5   "Etymology of the Name Nahash." Abiram Publications. April 19, 2006. https://www.abarim-publications.com/Meaning/Nahash.html.

- This word seems uncannily similar to helel, the Hebrew word translated to English as lucifer in Isaiah 14:12, which means bright and shiny one.

- I'm not sure why the translators used the wording they decided on; however, the point is that it looks like both words, nahash and helel, describe the same being.

❖ <u>Ezekiel 28:13–16:</u>

You were in Eden, the garden of God; Every precious stone was your covering: The sardius, topaz, and diamond, beryl, onyx, and jasper, sapphire, turquoise, and emerald with gold. The workmanship of your timbrels and pipes was prepared for you on the day you were created. You were the anointed cherub who covers; I established you; You were on the holy mountain of God; You walked back and forth in the midst of the fiery stones. You were perfect in your ways from the day you were created, till iniquity was found in you.

- Ezekiel 28:13–16 describes the same entity in Genesis 3 and Isaiah 14, which is satan.

- God initially assigned him to the Garden as an anointed covering cherub; however, he became lifted up in pride because of his beauty and started considering himself as important.

- He may have even partaken of the forbidden fruit in the Garden of Eden.

- He fell first; then, he got Adam and Eve to fall so he could infiltrate the human race and attack God out of jealousy.

- This fallen cherub started all of the competition that takes place among humanity today.

- Just as he did with Adam and Eve, he still uses the same strategy of deceptive thoughts to infiltrate people's lives.

What is the only way that satan can gain access to human beings? How does he do this?

_____
_____
_____
_____
_____

DISCUSSION:

It is noteworthy to remember that the Nephilim taught the people to interbreed, so they had to believe a lie and give access to the seed of the serpent. Similar corruption will happen again at the end of days; it's already started. The gateway for this demonic infiltration and corruption of human genetics is through deception, just like in Genesis. Many people will believe the enemy's lies and allow their bodies to be genetically compromised, which is why I emphasize the importance of being spiritually aware and taking action to build up your immune system.

Demons or disembodied spirits are territorial because they remain in the same area they were in before the flood. When the flood came, the hybrid people drowned and lost their bodies; however, their spirits are still on the earth in a parallel realm. It does not matter whether a spirit is underwater or on the land because they are in a different dimension. They are not restricted like we are. They have other parameters in the spirit realm. Getting humans to interbreed would allow these entities to enter the physical realm, which is why God stopped it with the flood. After the flood, David had to take out the giant races because human blood was compromised again.

There is not much information about demons in the Bible until Jesus came. When He arrived, the demonic spirits knew who He was. They also knew what Jesus could and couldn't do as the Son of Man. The unclean spirits did not want to be moved out of their area or sent into the torment of hell before it was time (Matthew 8:29). There was a specific timeline, so Jesus didn't send them to the pit during His earthly ministry; if He had, the Bible would have said so.

- ❖ Since spirit beings of all levels are shut out of this physical realm, the only way that they can have any kind of expression is to hijack human beings.

- ❖ <u>John 14:12 TPT:</u>

  I tell you this timeless truth: The person who follows Me in faith, believing in Me, will do the same mighty miracles that I do—even greater miracles than these because I go to be with My Father!

  - Jesus is the Son of God, but He came to the world as the Son of Man, operating in a man's body by the anointing of the Holy Spirit.

  - Therefore, He could tell the disciples that they could do the same works, including casting out demons.

  - After the disciples, Jesus sent 72 others out (Luke 10:1), and then He said that everyone who believes in Him would operate in the same power of the Holy Spirit.

  - He declared in John 14:12 that a day would come when we would do even greater works than He did.

What did Jesus promise those who follow Him in faith would be able to do?

_____

_____

_____

_____

_____

❖ Jesus did everything as the Son of Man. Even though He was the Son of God, He laid that aside and became a servant (Philippians 2:5–11) who did everything under the anointing of the Holy Spirit.

DISCUSSION:

Jesus went through life, as we all do, and was even baptized to fulfill all righteousness (Matthew 3:13–15). Jesus understood what it was like to be tempted by the devil (Matthew 4:1–11). He had to cast down the enemy's lies by using God's Word to resist satan in the wilderness, just like we do. He essentially fulfilled everything people would need and became the ultimate sacrifice. Through His life, Jesus taught us how to navigate spiritual warfare.

Why is it important to understand that Jesus did everything as the Son of Man?

_____
_____
_____
_____

THE MANIFOLD WISDOM OF GOD

DISCUSSION:

When Jesus went forth in the power of the Spirit, the demons recognized who He was, and they started to manifest. Until that point, for the most part, when people in the Bible would speak or act, we don't read about many demonic manifestations. Before Jesus, the influence of the spirit realm remained mainly behind the scenes.

- ❖ We have been given the name and the blood of Jesus; the finished work of the cross is now in effect (John 19:30). Today, we are commissioned to go forth and drive out devils, period.

- ❖ We are not supposed to argue with them, converse with them, investigate, or look for them; we are instructed to drive them out.

❖ **Matthew 10:7-8:**

And as you go, preach, saying, "The kingdom of heaven is at hand." Heal the sick, cleanse the lepers, raise the dead, cast out demons. Freely you have received, freely give.

- Believers are sent to preach the gospel.

- In response to that gospel message, the dead will be raised; the sick will be healed; there will be Jubilee—debt forgiveness, and sins will be forgiven.

- We will also see devils driven out of people. That's our assignment as the body of Christ.

❖ **Ephesians 3:9-11:**

And to make all see what is the fellowship of the mystery, which from the beginning of the ages has been hidden in God who created all things through Jesus Christ; to the intent that now the manifold wisdom of God might be made known by the church to the principalities and powers in the heavenly places, according to the eternal purpose which He accomplished in Christ Jesus our Lord.

- Jesus's crucifixion and resurrection destroyed the works of the devil behind the scenes.

- However, entities are still in place, ruling and reigning through world leaders.

- They appear to be unaffected by what has happened on the cross. That's why I explained to you their defeat will not be evident until we enforce the victory through the revelation of the manifold wisdom of God, expressed in Ephesians 3:9-11.

- The mystery is that as this wisdom is revealed through the church, it brings judgment to the powers of the air.

- Through the body of Christ, God will reveal Himself to the principalities, which will execute this judgment; this will not happen through an individual.

Read Ephesians 3:9-11. What is the manifold wisdom of God, and who will make it known?

_____

_____

_____

_____

_____

CORRECT VIEW OF SPIRITUAL WARFARE

DISCUSSION:

Today, we have an overabundance of deliverance teaching and ministries; however, the gospel didn't focus on that. Deliverance was never meant to be compartmentalized. When advancing the gospel, it is among other demonstrations, such as healing the sick and raising the dead. One is not more challenging to perform than the other.

When you encounter demons, you drive them out; you are not supposed to look for them or label your meetings. As such, you should see other manifestations of God's power in addition to deliverance.

- ❖ Even though deliverance is part of the gospel, Jesus didn't focus only on that one aspect; He preached and demonstrated the whole gospel message.

- ❖ <u>Matthew 16:21-23:</u>

    From that time Jesus began to show His disciples that He must go to Jerusalem, and suffer many things from the elders and chief priests and scribes, and be killed, and be raised the third day. Then Peter took Him aside and began to rebuke Him, saying, "Far be it from You, Lord; this shall not happen to You!" But He turned and said to Peter, "Get behind Me, Satan! You are an offense to Me, for you are not mindful of the things of God, but of the things of men."

    - In 2 Corinthians 10:5, we are admonished to cast down arguments and every false idea that comes against the knowledge of God.

    - The dialog between Jesus and Peter in Matthew 16:21-23 is a perfect example.

    - After Jesus expressed that He would be turned over to the authorities and crucified, Peter rebuked Him and said it wouldn't happen.

    - At that point, Jesus addressed him as satan and told him his ideas were not from God.

    - This is the proper way to look at spiritual warfare.

What is the correct way to look at spiritual warfare? How does this change your perspective?

___

DISCUSSION:

Everything I've shared with you is to establish a firm foundation based on the Word of God. It's not a complete study of the origins of spiritual warfare, which would take months. If you would like more information on this subject, you can get my three-volume *Holy Fire* set, which will explain many of these topics in greater detail. It is a three-book set, with about nine hundred pages, that discusses the origin and operation of the demonic and reveals how satan does not want us to walk in holiness and the holy fire.

As the church, we must be ready to punish all disobedience by fulfilling our obedience as a body, according to 2 Corinthians 10:6. You must look at what the Word of God precisely says and not make it something that it's not. I've made it very simple for you because it's not complicated at all. In the chapters ahead, I will show you how to fortify your walk with God so that you can see deliverance.

CHAPTER 5

THE TRUTH SETS CAPTIVES FREE

The Spirit of the Lord is upon Me, because He has anointed Me to preach the gospel to the poor; He has sent Me to heal the brokenhearted, to proclaim liberty to the captives and recovery of sight to the blind, to set at liberty those who are oppressed; To proclaim the acceptable year of the Lord.
—Luke 4:18–19

DISCUSSION:

The basis of the gospel message is found in Luke 4:18–19. Jesus is actually reading a prophecy about Himself from Isaiah (Isaiah 61:1–3). It says that The Holy Spirit anointed him to preach the gospel specifically to the poor. Jesus was sent to heal the brokenhearted, recover sight for the blind, and preach deliverance to the captives. If you're captive, then you need deliverance. Setting at liberty those who are oppressed means breaking shackles. Preaching the favorable year of the Lord refers to the fulfillment of Jubilee, which is debt forgiveness (Leviticus 25:10). This is the foundation of the gospel message.

DELIVERANCE IS NOT EXCLUSIVE

❖ **Mark 16:15–18 TPT:**
And He said to them, "As you go into all the world, preach openly the wonderful news of the gospel to the entire human

race! Whoever believes the good news and is baptized will be saved, and whoever does not believe the good news will be condemned. And these miracle signs will accompany those who believe: They will drive out demons in the power of My name. They will speak in tongues. They will be supernaturally protected from snakes and from drinking anything poisonous. And they will lay hands on the sick and heal them."

- The Spirit of the Lord was on Jesus to preach the gospel message and break the yokes of sickness and oppression off of people.

- He allowed the Holy Spirit to manifest through His life to do the works written in Luke 4:18-19.

- This is what ministry was meant to be. All of us are qualified to preach the good news.

- Mark 16:17 expresses that miraculous signs will follow those who believe or the believing ones.

- This verse refers to all of us, not just five-fold ministers.

- I don't know how certain aspects of ministry became exclusive for five-fold ministers because the gifts of the Spirit are for everybody. The Bible doesn't designate only certain people to operate in these gifts.

DISCUSSION:

To understand the five-fold, let's take a moment to look at the apostle Paul's life. He was chosen to be an apostle since birth, yet he spent much of his life working against God and killing Christians (Galatians 1:13–16). He didn't seem to have a choice because it was written that he would be an apostle. For half of Paul's life, he resisted God, and then he was arrested by the Lord on the road to Damascus. During this encounter, Paul recognized the Person in glistening clothes who spoke to him as Lord (Acts 9:1-6).

Paul called Jesus Lord, experienced conversion, and then started to fulfill his apostleship. He said in his writings that he was appointed as an apostle since birth, much earlier than the road to Damascus. Jesus essentially said, "I chose you. You didn't choose me." This means fivefold ministers are part of the church's foundation, which Christ sets and ordains; this differs from the gifts the Holy Spirit gives people as He wills (1 Corinthians 12:11).

- ❖ Ephesians 4:11-13 NLT:

    Now these are the gifts Christ gave to the church: the apostles, the prophets, the evangelists, and the pastors and teachers. Their responsibility is to equip God's people to do His work and build up the church, the body of Christ. This will continue until we all come to such unity in our faith and knowledge of God's Son that we will be mature in the Lord, measuring up to the full and complete standard of Christ.

    - In every generation, five-fold ministers are chosen by God. God sets them in the church like a jeweler places gems within a setting.

    - The idea is that they're part of God's plan and sent by Him; they don't appoint themselves.

    - You can see that Paul didn't have a choice. Jesus told him it was hard for him to kick against the goads (Acts 9:5). Goads were prods that would poke animals, such as cows, to move in a specific direction, gather together, or stay within their set boundaries.

    - Jesus addressed Paul this way because He wanted to guide him onto the right path.

❖ **John 15:16:**

You did not choose Me, but I chose you and appointed you that you should go and bear fruit, and that your fruit should remain, that whatever you ask the Father in My name He may give you.

❖ **1 Corinthians 12:7–11:**

But the manifestation of the Spirit is given to each one for the profit of all: for to one is given the word of wisdom through the Spirit, to another the word of knowledge through the same Spirit, to another faith by the same Spirit, to another gifts of healings by the same Spirit, to another the working of miracles, to another prophecy, to another discerning of spirits, to another different kinds of tongues, to another the interpretation of tongues. But one and the same Spirit works all these things, distributing to each one individually as He wills.

- The Holy Spirit is the One who gives out the gifts; each of us receives gifts according to the Spirit's discernment and will.

- Everyone has at least one of the gifts of the Spirit, which means that we all can and should operate in the supernatural.

- It's the same with driving out demons—all of us can do it.

- Ministry is not just for the five-fold ministers; the gospel message is to be preached by all believing ones.

- Notice there is no gift of casting out demons in 1 Corinthians 12:7–11 or anywhere else in the Bible.

- Jesus gave us all His name as believers to drive out demons (Mark 16:17).

- Deliverance is not complicated, but because this aspect of ministry has not been taught correctly, many people misunderstand it; therefore, it does not work for them.

What is the purpose of the five-fold ministry? Who is eligible to minister the gospel?

_____
_____
_____
_____
_____

Why is "casting out demons" not listed as a gift of the Spirit?

_____
_____
_____
_____
_____

❖ <u>Romans 10:17:</u>
So then faith comes by hearing, and hearing by the Word of God.

- We are all supposed to see healings, deliverances, and people raised from the dead.

- However, you won't see the results if you don't emphasize this through teaching the Scripture and meditating on the truth.

- If you concentrate on certain truths, you will see the manifestation.

- Many isolate specific subjects and may see results, but they leave out the rest of the gospel.

- The gospel message includes a variety of demonstrations.

- For example, in a crowd, some need deliverance, others need healing, some need debt cancellation, and someone may need to be raised from the dead. Some need good news because they're poor.

List the demonstrations that are included in the gospel message.

_____
_____
_____
_____
_____

Why don't some people see these demonstrations that follow the gospel?

_____

_____

_____

_____

_____

A GREATER COVENANT

DISCUSSION:

Why was the gospel such good news when Israel was supposed to be a nation that was blessed by God? According to Deuteronomy 28:1-14, obedient people of God would be the head, not the tail; they wouldn't have to borrow from anyone but would lend to people because they would own everything. The Scripture said that people from other nations would come and bow down to them. Their enemies would try to attack them from one way and end up fleeing in seven directions. The problem was that the people of Israel strayed away from God; however, in the New Testament, Jesus fulfilled all those promises of the old covenant.

- ❖ <u>Hebrews 8:8-10</u>:

    Because finding fault with them, He says: "Behold, the days are coming, says the Lord, when I will make a new covenant with the house of Israel and with the house of Judah—not according to the covenant that I made with their fathers in the day when I took them by the hand to lead them out of the land of

Egypt; because they did not continue in My covenant, and I disregarded them, says the Lord. For this is the covenant that I will make with the house of Israel after those days, says the Lord: I will put My laws in their mind and write them on their hearts; and I will be their God, and they shall be My people."

- The new covenant is a greater, better covenant with better promises.

- It is based on the blood of Jesus.

- The new covenant includes the manifestations of the gospel that we have been discussing.

- One of these manifestations is deliverance.

How does Hebrews 8:8–10 describe our new and better covenant with God?

_____

_____

_____

_____

_____

DISMANTLE STRONGHOLDS WITH TRUTH

DISCUSSION:

In a previous chapter, we explored 2 Corinthians 10:4–5. I recommend memorizing this passage, which describes the weapons of our warfare. These weapons are not carnal or physical, but they're mighty in the supernatural realm of God for pulling down strongholds. A stronghold is a fortress, which is a place where the enemy is holed up; it's a dwelling place. Picture the enemy as if they were hornets; then imagine destroying their nest so they scatter. That's the idea of spiritual warfare; you go to the enemy's stronghold and tear down their hiding place, exposing them to where they can no longer hide. The enemy is always trying to remain covert. Notice how most crime takes place at night, in the darkness; you get the idea. Pulling down strongholds is also like when the walls of Jericho fell, exposing the enemy within them; this is a visual image of what happens when you cast down arguments or thoughts that rise up against the knowledge of God.

- ❖ John 8:32 NLT:
  And you shall know the truth, and the truth will set you free.

  - Remember that the whole idea of warfare is to expose the enemy and forbid him to have walls to hide behind.

  - If you want successful deliverance in people, you must teach it this way.

  - In a service, when you dismantle the enemy by exposing him and people no longer have strongholds in their minds, deliverance will flow in the room.

❖ Deliverance takes place in every Warrior Notes service. I don't have to address the devil or pull people out. I just preach the gospel. As I speak the truth, it addresses and dismantles the enemy's strongholds in people.

❖ **Matthew 3:16-17:**

When He had been baptized, Jesus came up immediately from the water; and behold, the heavens were opened to Him, and He saw the Spirit of God descending like a dove and alighting upon Him. And suddenly a voice came from heaven, saying, "This is My beloved Son, in whom I am well pleased."

- I address people's arguments about certain truths in services by explaining them with Scripture.

- For example, some people do not believe in the Trinity of the Godhead.

- When you look at Matthew 3, the scenario where John the Baptist baptized Jesus, you can see that denying the Trinity is a ridiculous lie.

- When John baptized Jesus, the Holy Spirit descended on Him.

- Then the Father God spoke from Heaven saying, "This is my beloved Son, in whom I am well pleased." That voice was the God of Abraham, Isaac, and Jacob.

- The God and Father of our Lord Jesus Christ spoke from Heaven while Jesus was on the earth as the Son being baptized; Jesus didn't throw His voice up into the air and say that; it was the Father speaking.

- To drive the point home—the Father speaks from His throne while the Spirit of God is descending on Jesus, who was being baptized. How could you deny the Trinity?

- That's just one of many examples. I just cast down an argument. How? I stated the truth of the Bible. We are all called to speak the truth.

How do you cast down an argument that comes against the truth of God's Word?

_____

_____

_____

_____

_____

DISCUSSION:

Through Warrior Notes, people are sent out to preach the gospel. They are not just going out; they are being sent. You are already ordained by God, and He will honor your faithfulness. You are called to preach the favorable year of the Lord—the year of Jubilee—and to cast down strongholds by teaching Scripture.

Demons seek to get human beings to sin and walk away from God. That's what happened with Adam and Eve. They could not be deceived on their own; they had to be tricked. The serpent brought an argument to confuse Eve concerning what God said. He tried to make it sound like God was holding back from them when He wasn't (Genesis 3:1–7). This is real spiritual warfare.

When we come against the doctrinal issues, the lies of the enemy in people's minds, then those associated demons have to leave. People do not have demons in their spirits, but unclean spirits are around them, influencing their souls; they are being held captive. Once you explain to them that God didn't cause the traumatic events that allowed these demons to enter and get them to forgive and be healed, the demons leave because they have no stronghold left. We are supposed to destroy their strongholds; that's the bottom line.

- ❖ The strategy of demons is they exalt themselves above the knowledge of God. They want to deceive people because they know anyone who accepts their lies will be robbed of God's favor.

- ❖ **Psalm 91:13 ESV:**

    You will tread on the lion and the adder; the young lion and the serpent you will trample underfoot.

    - In Luke 10:18–19, Jesus said He saw satan fall like lightning from Heaven. He continued by stating that He gave believers authority to tread on serpents and scorpions.

    - Jesus promised that we would have power over all the enemy and that nothing would injure or harm us.

    - In Luke 10:18–19, Jesus was quoting from Psalms 91. Verse 13 states that you will tread on the lion and the adder—some translations say serpent, scorpion, the young lion, and the dragon, which is the serpent—and you shall trample them underfoot.

    - Psalms 91:10 says that no evil or disease can come near you, which is what Jesus was paraphrasing when He said, "Nothing shall be any means hurt you," in Luke 10:19.

- Jesus took what He learned from the Old Testament as a boy and quoted it. He transferred that revelation into the New Testament and taught that by invoking His name, we would see demons be driven out of people and trampled on.

- We have the authority to tread on serpents and scorpions and have power over the enemy.

What is the strategy that demons use to rob people of their favor?

_____

_____

_____

_____

What has Jesus given us authority to do to the enemy?

_____

_____

_____

_____

TRIUMPH THROUGH THE CROSS

DISCUSSION:

Jesus judged all evil spirits, but He didn't remove them. When driving unclean spirits out of people, Jesus didn't do what we see today in deliverance ministries, such as "sending demons to the pit." I'm not going to do anything that Jesus didn't do. As we discussed, I will certainly not go outside my boundaries because that will invite trouble.

❖ **Colossians 2:15 AMP:**

When He had disarmed the rulers and authorities [those supernatural forces of evil operating against us], He made a public example of them [exhibiting them as captives in His triumphal procession], having triumphed over them through the cross.

- When Jesus disarmed the rulers and authorities, He made a public display of them, having triumphed over them through the cross.

- In Colossians 2:15, Paul uses some of the same words to describe the levels of evil spirits he used in Ephesians 6, which we discussed.

- When Jesus went to the cross and triumphed over them, He bought us back; however, only those who believe through Jesus Christ are saved (Romans 10:9–10).

- Jesus defeated and judged all these evil spirits, rulers and authorities but didn't remove them; they're still there.

- He embarrassed them by making a public spectacle of them. That is the truth from the Word of God, on which we stand.

❖ **Exodus 14:13–14:**

And Moses said to the people, "Do not be afraid. Stand still, and see the salvation of the Lord, which He will accomplish for you today. For the Egyptians whom you see today, you shall see again no more forever. The Lord will fight for you, and you shall hold your peace."

- I recommend memorizing Exodus 14:13–14.

- This passage tells us not to be afraid.

- We are to stand still and see the salvation of the Lord, who will fight for us.

- This is another confirmation of what Paul expressed in Ephesians 6 about standing firm and being still.

- I believe Paul got his revelation from this passage in Exodus. As a Pharisee, he knew the Old Testament well, and there was no New Testament yet.

- The idea here is that the Lord has already given us victory and endowed us with all the weapons we need.

- Our armor is defensive; therefore, the Lord will execute our victory by fighting for us.

- These verses do not say we're supposed to initiate a fight; we are instructed to stand.

- The Lord will fight your battles, so hold your peace and stand still.

❖ You must understand the correction that, as the church, we are not obtaining something; we already have it. Now, we are defending and protecting what we were given.

❖ If you look at how Paul approaches this, it's vastly different than what's being portrayed as spiritual warfare today. Many people encounter the backlash and negative experiences from attempting spiritual battles because they are not staying within the proper boundaries or respecting authority.

Why do many people experience backlash from attempting spiritual warfare?

_____

_____

_____

_____

_____

What is the correct posture for warring in the spirit realm?

_____

_____

_____

_____

_____

DISCUSSION:

Many lack understanding regarding what Jesus accomplished for humanity through the cross. As mentioned several times, individuals can drive out the earthbound demons, the serpents, and the scorpions that Luke 10:19 refers to. Even though Jesus triumphed over the higher entities on the cross, these must only be dealt with through the local church, as the Holy Spirit leads.

BIBLICAL MINISTRY

DISCUSSION:

Biblical ministry begins with an apostle being sent into an area. Once that apostle is established there, they start a work. The prophet co-labors with the apostle by speaking from the other realm, giving insight, and opening up the heavenly realms. Then, the evangelist goes out into the community and gathers people to hear the gospel message. At that point, teachers and pastors are set over the local body; pastors can also be teachers.

Once a work is established, the apostle continues to go out, starting new works. Then the prophet comes in, opening up the heavens and prophesying the word of the Lord, which will involve the will of God for that area. Then, the evangelist goes out into the streets again, gathering people, telling them about Jesus, and bringing them in. Once they hear the gospel message and are saved, pastors and teachers collaborate locally to mentor and disciple them. This process repeats itself as they continue to expand. This is how warfare should be going on locally; it is the order God set up, and I wish it would be followed more. It's so simple. Warfare and deliverance are very easy to understand. As the body of Christ, we must get back on track and stick to the proper course established for us.

What is God's order for starting a new work in a region?

CHAPTER 6

OLD TESTAMENT FRAMEWORK FOR DELIVERANCE

For the Lord your God is He who goes with you, to fight for you against your enemies, to save you.
—Deuteronomy 20:4

DISCUSSION:

I hope you now understand more about your enemy and what you are contending with. Knowing what demons really are and their mode of operation simplifies deliverance for you. The revelations I received when I was with Jesus in Heaven concerning spiritual warfare were clearly defined in Scripture, but honestly, I had not previously heard much teaching about it. I realized that most people were just as much in the dark as I was about this topic. In the chapters ahead, we will continue to build upon the foundation that has been laid by examining more Scriptures.

As mentioned, New Testament leaders, including Jesus Himself, were educated in the old covenant through the Old Testament Scriptures. Jesus was brought up as a Jewish boy who had to memorize Scripture because that was part of their culture (Luke 2:46–47). Likewise, Paul was a Pharisee who was an expert in the Law (Philippians 3:4–5). He was a theologian who understood the Old Testament, inside and out. He supernaturally received revelation from Jesus Christ; however, all the New Testament Scripture was still being written. The point is that you will often see references from the Old Testament in the writings of the New Testament. Even many of Jesus's teachings included almost word-for-word quotes from the Old Testament.

❖ The Lord showed me that if I would seek out the Scripture as treasure, I would find the truth about everything.

What was the source of Jesus's and Paul's revelations? And how can you find the truth about anything?

_____
_____
_____
_____
_____

GOD FIGHTS FOR YOU AND ESTABLISHES YOUR PATH

DISCUSSION:

We must never forget that we are not fighting on our own. As we previously discussed, Jesus was sent to do the Father's will and encountered the enemy on the way; He never sought out warfare or the devil. The demons manifested themselves on the way and would talk to Him. The framework for this understanding can be observed in the Old Testament. When the Lord would speak to Moses or the prophets and the people obeyed His word, God would fight their enemies and give them victory. For example, in Deuteronomy 20:1–4, the Lord told Moses that when Israel had to go to battle, the troops should not be afraid because the Lord their God would go with them, giving them victory over their enemies.

- ❖ **James 1:13–15 KJV:**

  Let no man say when he is tempted, "I am tempted of God"; for God cannot be tempted by evil, neither tempteth He any man. But every man is tempted, when he is drawn away of his own lust, and enticed. Then, when lust hath conceived, it bringeth forth sin: and sin, when it is finished, bringeth forth death.

  - The mindset of the New Testament is not going out to fight a physical battle but understanding that the Lord is with us; our warfare and the weapons God gave us are spiritual.

  - The demonic entities that we wrestle with manifest themselves through people.

  - Demons gain access to individuals by infiltrating their thoughts, changing their minds, and influencing their desires.

  - If left unchecked, these demons will eventually deceive their victims and trick them into sinning, as the serpent did to Adam and Eve.

  - Once a person sins, the enemy has an open door to trap them in bondage.

  - When people are deceived or convinced of lies, demons then put shackles on them. At that point, they are demonized and need help.

- ❖ Demonized people need the message of the gospel preached to them and to have the demons cast out of them; in other words, they need deliverance.

- ❖ Just as God defeated the physical enemies of His people in the Old Testament, through Jesus Christ, He has given us victory over the demonic.

Describe the process demons use to gain access to individuals, according to James 1:13–15.

_____

_____

_____

_____

DISCUSSION:

God is faithful to make your pathway obvious so you will not miss it. One of the goals of this book is to show you that there is a set path for you. When you're in a forest with an established pathway, it's so clear that going off the trail is difficult. That means it's well-used and well-defined, which is why I called this book *Deliverance Made Easy*.

When I encountered Jesus in Heaven, I was shown my life and the messages I was supposed to teach. He clearly gave me the topics, which is why you hear all this revelation from Warrior Notes. For forty-five minutes, Jesus stood with me and taught me the Scriptures; however, it seemed like a week of teaching. I was undergoing an operation that was less than an hour, but it seemed like I was gone much longer because there are no clocks in Heaven or reference to time. It just seemed like it went on and on and on. He established me on the pathway of my life. It was so well defined that when I came back, it took a long time to convince me that what I was shown hadn't physically happened yet.

After I visited Heaven, I endured warfare for years. I suffered many hardships from that time until 2016 when I recorded my first show on Sid Roth. Shortly afterward, in 2017, I retired from Southwest Airlines. During that time, I had many physical problems, especially my sinuses and ears, so that I could barely fly. The pain was indescribable.

Many realities I experienced in Heaven had not happened when I returned to earth, even though I knew they were true. There was such a struggle at times. It took many years for me to process what happened during my visitation in 1992. I could not write the book *Heavenly Visitation* until 2015. I published it in 2016 and then was on TV. It took a lot of time for what I was shown to be integrated into my mind and my physical body. Other supernatural events happened to me, just like they probably have to you. God answered prayers and moved in my life. Yet I could only dream of the revelation of God's plans shown to me being fulfilled in my life, although I knew they were true. Much of it slipped my memory after a while, so when I wrote the book, it helped to bring it all back to the forefront.

I shared my journey to show you that I had to go through a process where God had to manifest my deliverance and come through for me. From 1992 through 2015, the Lord worked the revelations into my life. In 2016, I started to be established in all these truths. A war went on just to write that first book, which took me a year and a half. All I was doing was documenting what the Lord taught me on the other side and what happened in my heavenly visitation. You would think that would be an easy task, but I dealt with so much warfare that I struggled to sit down and write. The devil did not want that book to come out and certainly didn't want me on TV. Essentially, he has tried to undermine everything concerning Warrior Notes every step of the way.

Many people have seen what God has done and how I learned to trust in the Lord. Because of this, they have become acquainted with Warrior Notes and me. The testimony of Psalms 40 truly happened to me. The fruit of it all is that the deliverance that God did for me has become part of the experience of people around me. That is what will happen to you too. God will come through for you. You will be acquainted with His power and the deliverance of His arm grabbing and pulling you out. Then, you will see the enemy leave very quickly. He will vacate when you show up because you have already gained victory.

❖ The Lord established my goings, just as it says in Scripture. He put a song in my mouth to give praise unto God. I was pulled out of a horrible pit, shown the right way to live in Heaven, and sent back to the earth.

❖ I believe you will experience the Lord's strong arm in your life; it will be just as powerful and effective as it was for me.

❖ When the Lord has won you over, the enemy knows it and flees.

❖ **Psalms 40:1–3 KJV:**

I waited patiently for the Lord; and He inclined unto me and heard my cry. He brought me up also out of an horrible pit, out of the miry clay, and set my feet upon a rock, and established my goings. And He hath put a new song in my mouth, even praise unto our God: many shall see it, and fear, and shall trust in the Lord.

- The psalmist testified that God delivered him when he cried out to the Lord and waited patiently for Him.

- Essentially, the lesson that we learn here is that we stand.

- As it says in Ephesians 6:13, when we've done everything, we must stand and wait patiently, knowing that God will incline His ear and hear us.

- We must be confident that the Lord will answer and pull us out of the pit. Picture the miry clay, like quicksand, where your feet get stuck. Envision the Lord pulling you out of that and setting you on a solid foundation, the rock in this passage.

- Know that God will establish your goings; in other words, God ordained a clear pathway for you, which He will set you on.

Read Psalm 40:1-3. What will the Lord do if we wait patiently and cry out to Him?

_____

_____

_____

_____

_____

THE ENEMY FLEES FROM THOSE WHO HAVE SIDED WITH GOD

DISCUSSION:

Another aspect of the framework of how deliverance worked among the people of the Old Testament is found in Psalm 68:1-3. The God of the Old Testament is the same God of the New Testament. The New Testament was written from the Old with Jesus being the fulfillment (Matthew 5:17). The Holy Spirit implemented the covenant that Jesus cut through His blood (Hebrews 10:15-18). I encourage you to meditate on these Scriptures, building up your frame of mind, and you will effortlessly see deliverance happen not only in your own life but in the lives of others.

You won't even have to fast or pray necessarily. I'm not saying that fasting and prayer are not important; these are necessary for every believer. However, you should be thoroughly convinced and understand the ways of God, knowing that He will arise and scatter His enemies, which are your enemies. This is God's way of life, not something you must obtain by doing something special. When you build yourself up by meditating on these Scriptures, you will see God deliver people.

- ❖ The enemy will vacate when he knows you're fully convinced. He knows he has to leave. With this revelation, you don't need to consider yourself a deliverance minister. The demons manifest when you become established in who you are in the Spirit.

When you understand what God has done for you, you become settled in it, and the enemy opts out of the battle. With Jesus, demons knew they had to leave, so they just said, "Are you going torment us before our time?" They didn't argue whether or not they would have to leave. They already knew they would have to, but they didn't want to be sent to the pit or out of their assigned area (Mark 5:10).

Demonic spirits have worked hard to develop a network in each neighborhood, city, state, and country. It messes everything up when you encounter strongmen and send them out of the area. When you address them, it sets them back, sometimes years, in the process of what they've been doing in that city. As the body of Christ, we want to do this as much as possible.

The demons tried to negotiate with Jesus because they were doing damage control. Scripture doesn't say He sent them out of the area; however, it also doesn't say you can't do so. You can't send them to torment until it's their time (Matthew 8:29); the defined time appears to be at the end of this age when the angel comes and throws satan into the lake of fire (Revelation 20:10). The enemy is already judged up until that point; we are supposed to be enforcing the victory that we have through Jesus Christ by driving them out. So we can drive them out of their territory or domain. The Bible doesn't say we can't do that. The boundary is that we cannot send them to the pit to be tormented before their time. It is essential to rehearse these Scriptures.

❖ **Psalm 68:1–3:**

Let God arise, let His enemies be scattered; Let those also who hate Him flee before Him. As smoke is driven away, so drive them away; As wax melts before the fire, so let the wicked perish at the presence of God. But let the righteous be glad; Let them rejoice before God; Yes, let them rejoice exceedingly.

- Psalm 68:1 says to let those who hate God flee before Him. You will see that happen when any demons attack your life.

- When you have taken sides with God, the enemy that hates God will hate you, too. You shouldn't take it personally.

- The Scripture says that when this happens, the enemy will become like smoke that's just driven away and like wax that melts before the fire.

- The psalmist describes what will happen to your adversaries, who are also God's enemies. He said, "Let the wicked perish at the presence of God."

- The righteous, which is you and me, will be glad and rejoice before God exceedingly. We will see the victory.

How does the enemy respond when you take sides with God?

_____
_____
_____
_____
_____

Why shouldn't you take it personally when the enemy attacks?

_____

_____

_____

_____

_____

THE CHURCH'S RESPONSIBILITY

DISCUSSION:

In every area, the church is responsibility for cutting off the enemy. Whether a body of believers gathering in a house or a building, we agree to break up the enemy's supply in specific geographic regions and cut off their communication. We can command confusion to come into the enemy's camp (Psalm 55:9).

You can stop demons' supply by starving them. Don't give them any response or satisfaction, which would allow them to grow. Disembodied spirits gain power by feeding off people's souls. You starve them by preventing them from having any satisfaction or fulfillment by being close to a human being. When demons do not have a human host, they go into arid places and suffer. That is why they are seeking a body where they can live. Instead, send them to arid areas where they dry up.

❖ Micah 5:9 KJV:

Thine hand shall be lifted up upon thine adversaries, and all thine enemies shall be cut off.

- We know that what is said in the Old Testament is truth.

- The revelation about Jesus, His fulfillment, and the implementation of the new covenant builds upon the truth of the Old Testament.

- Jesus Christ fulfilled the demands of the Old Testament and the law.

- We must understand that through Him, we have victory over all our adversaries, and the enemy shall be cut off.

- I want to assure you that we have the authority and the ability to cut off the demons' strength and their ability to operate.

What is the church's responsibility when dealing with the enemy?

_____
_____
_____
_____
_____

CHAPTER 7

JESUS PAID FOR YOUR FREEDOM

And it shall come to pass in that day, that his burden shall be taken away from off thy shoulder, and his yoke from off thy neck, and the yoke shall be destroyed because of the anointing.
—Isaiah 10:27 KJV

DISCUSSION:

In the New Testament, Jesus fulfilled many Old Testament prophecies, including those Isaiah declared concerning the Messiah. We need to memorize and meditate on these powerful Scriptures, some of which we will discuss in this chapter. We must let them become part of us because they will help us fight the enemy so that we may see people delivered.

As you read and study the revelation in this chapter, I believe you will experience your own deliverance. The anointing and power of impartation are here, and demons must leave you alone. However, that is not the only goal; you are called to operate in this same anointing wherever you go, so that the enemy screams, gives up, and leaves before you even say anything. The ultimate goal for Warrior Notes Ministry is discipleship.

❖ As the body and church of the Lord Jesus Christ, we are supposed to operate in His authority on the earth, which means we should drive out demons as He did. It is straightforward.

❖ **Matthew 10:8:**

Heal the sick, cleanse the lepers, raise the dead, cast out demons. Freely you received, freely give.

- Just to be clear, I want to see you completely delivered.

- My desire is that the enemy leaves your life and no longer has any power over you.

- You are meant to walk in the victory that Jesus has given us.

- However, the fruit of this would be for you to turn around and do the same thing for others, which is what the church is supposed to be doing.

What happens when we walk in the victory that Jesus has given us?

_____
_____
_____
_____
_____

What does Matthew 10:8 instruct us to do?

_____
_____
_____
_____
_____

THE GOSPEL IS FREELY GIVEN

DISCUSSION:

Isaiah 10:27 tells us that the anointing will destroy yokes and burdens. Jesus Christ is the Anointed One, so the burdens and yokes are removed when He shows up. This means you won't have to carry them anymore. Sometimes, when people experience a breakthrough, they feel the manifestation of a weight lift off their shoulders. When a yoke is destroyed, it can never be fixed or put back on you; it's permanent.

What bothers me the most about some of today's so-called deliverance ministries is that people must pay to attend their meetings to get delivered. People have told me that they have been charged to listen to spiritual warfare seminars and then had to pay extra for deliverance prayer. Some ministers charge additional fees for personal deliverance sessions. I disassociate myself from all ministers and ministries that charge; there are many.

You should never feel pressured to give in an offering, as if under coercion, even to meet a ministry's expenses. Warrior Notes will never pressure people to give, even if we have costs. I tell everybody that the partners have already paid for the conferences and other ministries because I want to remove that pressure from those attending. I would never want anyone to give because they felt forced to do so; that completely goes against Scripture.

Sadly, most ministries manipulate people to increase offerings. Some even charge at the door. Others, even if they let you in for free, emphasize the amount the meeting costs. They may phrase it as raising funds, but to me, it is just like charging. I've been in meetings where they prolong the offering so that people feel compelled to give just to get on with the service. I've seen some practices that I don't think any of the apostles or biblical leaders would ever approve of.

There are times when it is appropriate to charge for a service. For example, we charge a small cost at the Warrior Notes School of

Ministry for those who can pay because it is a legitimate university degree. It is appropriate to charge for college credit because we have to pay our staff to run the school. The courses, which include technology, are done with excellence, and it costs money to do that. I spent hundreds and hundreds of dollars per credit hour for my degree, but I ensure that never happens for our students at the School of Ministry. We keep the costs very minimal, so it is affordable.

The demons love it when you overemphasize them. They also love it when you charge for something that should be free. Some expenses are understandable, but you shouldn't be paying for your deliverance or prayer. The same applies to every aspect of the gospel, yet deliverance ministry has been severely abused in this way. I want to know why people are being charged for ministry. If God has sent you, He will bless and prosper you and pay for it supernaturally. Jesus didn't charge, yet He did take offerings. He had a money bag, which had a lot of money in it (John 13:29). The money had to get into the bag somehow. The Bible doesn't specifically say, but it is implied that some individuals followed Jesus around and financed Him. Later, others financed the apostles too. This is God's way of doing it.

- ❖ Second Corinthians 8-9 are not very popular chapters of the Bible. These passages teach that you don't have to give if you don't want to; you should give only out of joy and for the right reasons.

- ❖ **1 Corinthians 9:18:**

  What is my reward then? That when I preach the gospel, I may present the gospel of Christ without charge, that I may not abuse my authority in the gospel.

  - Everything that we've been given through Jesus Christ was provided without charge.

  - It was costly to Jesus and the Father, so it wasn't free; however, the gospel was given at no cost.

- Paul did accept offerings, but he said that we shouldn't give out manipulation.

- Nobody should be coerced into giving; it should be something we want to do out of joy (2 Corinthians 9:7–8).

- God loves a cheerful giver.

What should be our attitude and motive when giving to the work of the Lord?

_____

_____

_____

_____

_____

DELIVERANCE IS PERMANENT

DISCUSSION:

Demonic yokes are removed and destroyed because of the anointing. The anointing cannot be bought or manipulated; it's something God freely gives out and is permanent. However, regardless of whether or not you paid for it, you should be delivered permanently. Amazingly, many have been charged for deliverance seminars and even paid extra for the materials and prayer to find that their freedom was not permanent. Some people will do anything to be delivered—even pay significant sums—then when you talk to them, the demons have come back.

The anointing on the Messiah and given to us, the body of Christ, is the yoke-destroying anointing. I must emphasize this because God said that in the day of the Messiah, which is now, the yoke will be removed from our necks and destroyed because of the anointing. The anointing is the Anointed One—the Messiah, the Deliverer, period. Jesus gave deliverance to us for free, and it's permanent. So, if the ministry we received is temporary, we must look at what's really going on. The problem is that people must be taught the simplicity of deliverance and understand that God is with them.

❖ <u>Joshua 1:5:</u>

No man shall be able to stand before you all the days of your life; as I was with Moses, so I will be with you. I will not leave you or forsake you.

- Because God is with you, your enemies are now His enemies. They will not be able to stand before Him.

- When you invoke the name of Jesus, use the power of His blood, and talk about the covenant, demons will leave because there is no contest (Mark 16:17).

- Temporary deliverance did not happen with Jesus; it was always permanent. The demons understood that He was sent and knew why He was on the earth; they asked Him, "Have you come to destroy us before our time?"

- Jesus did destroy the works of the enemy on the cross, so now it is finished (1 John 3:8; John 19:30). The works of the enemy have been destroyed, which means that all we're doing is showing up as ambassadors.

- The point is that you don't have to spend a whole weekend and pay a lot of money to learn deliverance.

How does the revelation of God always being with you help you understand deliverance?

DISCUSSION:

When you receive ministry to be delivered from demonic oppression, it should be free and permanent. That is not happening with most ministries today, so I need to address it. God has promised permanent deliverance through the anointing of the Holy One, the Messiah. When you meet Him, He will tell you His blood was enough. Through Him, there will never be a time when a demon doesn't leave. I know this to be true because I met Jesus and talked to Him before I was sent back. The Person who is our God never takes no for an answer. If He says something, it is established and will come to pass.

Jesus will have His way. If you are in the way, He will move you out of the way. You will be asked to step aside if you do not side with Him. That's just how Jesus is; He will tell you that his blood was enough. You will not go to Jesus and tell Him that you told a demon to leave, and it wouldn't listen to the name of Jesus. You will not go to Jesus and say to Him that you commanded a demon to leave and it would not listen to the name of Jesus. You cannot make the excuse that it did not obey; it will not happen. You will not say, "It did not work," because Jesus will tell you, "My blood was enough. My name is enough." He would tell you that He's not returning to be crucified again. There's nothing more He can do.

- ❖ <u>John 19:30:</u>

    So when Jesus had received the sour wine, He said, "It is finished!" And bowing His head, He gave up His spirit.

    - When Jesus hung on the cross, right before He died, He said, "It is finished."

    - The word He spoke was "*tetelestai*,"[6] which means *paid in full*; there are no amendments and nothing left to do about the enemy.

    - Jesus's death on the cross has legally processed the transaction.

    - Yet to require people to pay for it is wrong; you cannot do that if you are sent.

- ❖ Every covenant promise in the Bible has already been paid; the cost to get the message to you was significant.

- ❖ <u>Isaiah 43:2:</u>

    When you pass through the waters, I will be with you; And through the rivers, they shall not overflow you. When you walk through the fire, you shall not be burned, nor shall the flame scorch you.

    - Isaiah 43:2 states that God guarantees protection from the enemy for His people.

    - Whether it's water or fire, you will be completely protected.

    - We must have this mindset when encountering the enemy; it's the whole idea of Psalms 91.

---

6 "G5055 - teleō - Strong's Greek Lexicon (nkjv)." Blue Letter Bible. Accessed 23 Jul, 2023. https://www.blueletterbible.org/lexicon/g5055/nkjv/tr/0-1/

❖ **Isaiah 54:17 AMP:**

"No weapon that is formed against you will succeed; And every tongue that rises against you in judgment you will condemn. This [peace, righteousness, security, and triumph over opposition] is the heritage of the servants of the Lord, and this is their vindication from Me," says the Lord.

- Isaiah 54:17 is another verse that I recommend memorizing.

- It says that anything manufactured by the enemy to come against you will not prosper; it will not succeed.

- Every person who speaks a lie or a judgment against you will be condemned.

- Here, the prophet Isaiah prophesied about the future. All these promises are the heritage of the Lord's servants.

- Your deliverance and everything that you get from God is free.

- If something is your heritage, it means that you inherit it freely.

- In this verse, the Lord says that He will vindicate you.

Explain how God guarantees protection from the enemy, according to Isaiah 43:2 and Isaiah 54:17.

_____
_____
_____
_____
_____

What does heritage mean in Isaiah 54:7?

_____

_____

_____

_____

TRAFFICKING DEMONS

DISCUSSION:

I've watched a lot of deliverance sessions from different individuals, and at first, I didn't discern what was going on; it took a while. I witnessed one case where I thought the ministry was legitimate, but I eventually discerned a familiar spirit in operation after a while. I began to observe that some of these individuals claiming to minister deliverance were, in fact, trafficking demons; they were not really having people delivered. I saw manifestations that appeared genuine, but then, suddenly, the demons jumped from one person to another. The so-called minister operated as a master of ceremonies, trafficking the demons, so that they manifested and appeared as if they were being cast out.

I repeatedly watched these deliverance videos and clearly saw the demons going from one person to another. The Lord called this is a revolving door. In other words, the same thing keeps happening. These meetings took place in large churches in different countries; they only emphasized deliverance, but it was more like voodoo or a séance. They repeatedly trafficked demons through revolving doors in the spirit realm.

Many deliverance ministries are a scam and work with familiar spirits. I found out later that many of these ministers were previously involved with witchcraft ceremonies. You would probably know all these people. Through these ceremonies, they were initiated and given supernatural powers from demons that cooperated to put on a show. I was surprised because I was initially deceived; I thought they were legitimate until I couldn't ignore that something was wrong. I checked into it with local ministers and pastors in the countries to find that everyone had the same story.

I exposed what occurs in many deliverance ministries because the enemy wants to deceive people; he doesn't want you to know the truth about him. For the devil to have power, he has to hide the truth. Many things are happening today that we call ministry, but it is not the ministry of the Holy Spirit. It doesn't seem like anybody's speaking up about it. However, I will do what the Lord tells me to do. I want you to be aware of fraudulent ministry so that you can let the Lord speak to you; it doesn't have to take you as long as it took me to figure this out.

I have distanced myself from many ministries because they're operating in familiar spirits. Sometimes, the ministers that seem to get promoted on TV are not doing well spiritually, but you wouldn't know it. Their ministries are a revolving door, creating the appearance of deliverance.

In the book of Acts, Paul dealt with familiar spirits in people following him. In Acts 16:16–18, a woman acted like she was promoting the gospel by telling the crowds to listen to these men tell them the way to salvation. Perhaps he thought something was not right initially but didn't address it for a couple of days. After three days, Paul heard clearly from the Lord that this was not the Holy Spirit but a familiar spirit in operation. At that point, he addressed that demon and cast it out. That demon had been trying to preserve its position in her and the city. If you look at what happened, that lady had brought great wealth to businesspeople, so they got mad when she lost her power (Acts 16:19–24). They wanted the apostles to leave the city because of the so-called damage they had done, so the city turned against them because they negatively impacted their finances.

How do scam ministries work with familiar spirits? Why do we need to understand this?

_____

_____

_____

_____

_____

❖ **1 Timothy 6:10 AMP:**

For the love of money [that is, the greedy desire for it and the willingness to gain it unethically] is a root of all sorts of evil, and some by longing for it have wandered away from the faith and pierced themselves [through and through] with many sorrows.

- When you investigate many ministries today, you will discover they are centered on making money. That's why you'll see them charging and pushing offerings.

- I believe that this information will help you to discern.

- My desire is for you to develop your understanding in the area of deliverance for yourself and other people.

- I want you to have a firm foundation of what the Word of God says and be aware that the enemy does not want ministers operating in deliverance the right way.

- The devil will attack ministers and ministries in an attempt to render them ineffective. I'm making it very simple so you can discern and see clearly.

What does the love of money result in, according to 1 Timothy 6:10?

_____
_____
_____
_____
_____

CHAPTER 8

THE BATTLE IS ALREADY WON

*The Lord thy God in the midst of thee is
mighty; He will save, He will rejoice over
thee with joy; He will rest in His love,
He will joy over thee with singing.*
—Zephaniah 3:17 KJV

DISCUSSION:

We discussed the enemy's corruption of deliverance ministry with money and began uncovering his mode of operation through familiar spirits disguised as ministry of the Holy Spirit. I've noticed that many ministers have taken on these spirits, so you must be careful these days and understand that there should not be an overemphasis on deliverance or any one aspect of the gospel. I will continue to expose how the enemy works behind the scenes in the light of God's truth so that you can recognize his schemes and avoid pitfalls.

❖ Isaiah 61:1-2:

The Spirit of the Lord God is upon Me, because the Lord has anointed Me to preach good tidings to the poor; He has sent Me to heal the brokenhearted, to proclaim liberty to the captives, and the opening of the prison to those who are bound; to proclaim the acceptable year of the Lord, and the day of vengeance of our God; to comfort all who mourn.

- We are called to preach and demonstrate the gospel message described in Isaiah 61:1-2, just like Jesus did.

- The gospel message has different aspects, with deliverance being just one.

- As you walk with the Lord, Isaiah 54:17 promises that no weapon formed against you will prosper, and your vindication will come from the Lord.

- In light of this truth, we must recognize the weapons of the enemy when they form, especially the ones that come disguised as blessings from God.

When the Spirit of the Lord comes on a person, what is the fruit according to Isaiah 61:1–2?

_____

_____

_____

_____

A TRANSACTION WITH THE DEVIL

DISCUSSION:

As previously discussed, Paul had to separate himself from the woman following him (Acts 16:16–19). She promoted their ministry by saying, "Listen, these people are of God." However, she was a witch who, in reality, was masking a familiar spirit, hoping that Paul wouldn't cast it out. That evil spirit knew that Paul went from city to city, so perhaps it was hoping to lie low and act like a supporter until he left. It wanted to stay in that woman and continue to collect money for fortune telling.

Fortune telling is performed by witches who traffic familiar spirits. People come to them and pay to have their future told. It works because the evil spirits obtain information from the spirit realm for the witches to tell their clients. These demons get information from familiar spirits who know the person's family. The clients are often amazed when a fortune teller reveals something about them that a stranger would never know. Afterward, the witch says something about the future to hook the person and insert some curse to ensnare them. For example, they may tell them the same disease that killed their father will come upon them unless they deal with it. Then the scared person pays the witch to eliminate this curse and prevent the prediction from happening.

When you pay a fortune teller or a witch, a transaction takes place. In other words, if you offer money to deal with an evil spirit to prevent something terrible from happening, you have unknowingly made an agreement with the demonic realm; this opens the door to their influence in other ways. You wouldn't think that witchcraft could creep into the church; however, these transactions with witches and warlocks happen thousands of times per day where people pay and go through the process I just described.

Familiar spirits stand beside mediums, who are witches or warlocks; these spirits go and get information, come back at the speed of light, and give the information to the witch. When the witches share it with their clients, they are surprised. When they are open, the witch may say something futuristic or give a fortune; then, they will share bad news concerning what's working against them. People often fall right into the trap and pay the witch or warlock to prevent the curse; however, they unknowingly make a deal with the devil, which may seem good initially but never ends well. That happens often in Hollywood and is why many people rise into what they call stardom and are later struck with tragedy.

❖ **2 Corinthians 2:11 AMP:**

To keep satan from taking advantage of us; for we are not ignorant of his schemes.

- It's disturbing how much I have seen witchcraft creep into the church, especially among the prophetic and deliverance ministries.

- Have you noticed that when there are meetings with several guest prophets, you must pay to get in? Some are so bold that you have to pay if you want a word, or a preferred seat where you might get a word or to have a meal with the man or woman of God.

- This type of corruption seems to be common among specific sectors. It mainly has to do with getting words and deliverance.

- Many of these ministers work in the same ways that witches work.

- You can pay a witch or warlock to work with the familiar spirits to accomplish anything you want, whether it's good or bad.

- I find it interesting that more people don't see through this.

How do we prevent the enemy from taking advantage of us, according to 2 Corinthians 2:11? What is the scheme of the enemy that Dr. Zadai described in this chapter?

_____

_____

_____

_____

_____

❖ Acts 8:18–23:

> And when Simon saw that through the laying on of the apostles' hands the Holy Spirit was given, he offered them money, saying, "Give me this power also, that anyone on whom I lay hands may receive the Holy Spirit." But Peter said to him, "Your money perish with you, because you thought that the gift of God could be purchased with money! You have neither part nor portion in this matter, for your heart is not right in the sight of God. Repent therefore of this your wickedness, and pray God if perhaps the thought of your heart may be forgiven you. For I see that you are poisoned by bitterness and bound by iniquity."

- Jesus, Paul, and the apostles never took money for preferred seating, words, or deliverance.

- Nobody in the Bible ever paid to get demons cast out.

- Simon was a warlock who offered to pay the apostles for the power to lay hands on people to receive the Holy Spirit.

- The apostle Peter said, "Your money perish with you!" In other words, he told Simon that he would be destroyed with his money. That might not have sounded very nice, but that's how it was. Can you imagine if I said that today?

How did Peter respond to the sorcerer who offered to pay for the power of the Holy Spirit?

_____
_____
_____
_____

FREELY DELIVERED THROUGH CHRIST

DISCUSSION:

Nobody wants to admit they're wrong, but many will find out they are wrong when they reach Heaven, but why wait? This is what happened to me. I was wrong about many things; therefore, when I got to Heaven, I was corrected. Although I had Bibles everywhere in my house, I was supernaturally given the word of God. The Lord showed me that He fights our enemies; He's already defeated the devil, so essentially, He's broken the yoke of bondage off of everyone. Now, captives are set free through the preaching of the gospel message and proclaiming this liberty. Deliverance comes through the gospel, not by charging people for counseling, prayer or words.

Scripture doesn't say that deliverance comes from laying on of hands; it says that you lay hands on the sick, and they will recover

(Mark 16:17–18). It does not say, "Lay hands on the demon-possessed, and they shall be delivered." Many processes are taking place in ministry that are contrary how the Bible teaches. If the enemy is defeated but still influences people, we should look at what is really happening. I've noticed that ministries that charge for deliverance do not seem to have permanent results; as previously mentioned, it's a revolving door. It's the same with the prophetic ministry, where many have paid to meet with a prophet, most of the so-called predictions didn't come to pass. The people just ended up out of money.

Again, none of the apostles charged. In fact, they didn't have prayer or prophecy lines; they didn't call people out either. These practices developed in recent years; they were not part of the original church. They laid hands on and prayed for the sick, but it was mostly the elders who did that (James 5:14–15); not the five-fold ministers. The book of Acts mentions a waiter named Stephen, who wasn't an apostle, yet did notable miracles (Acts 6:2–8).

The bottom line is that deliverance has been given to us freely by Jesus Christ (Matthew 10:7–8); we are told to proclaim freedom to the captives (Luke 4:18–19). And if a spirit manifests, so be it; however, we shouldn't look for a manifestation. I look for the exit that the enemy leaves through, preferring that he go quietly and never return; that is deliverance. The announcement of the gospel's good news makes demons uncomfortable with staying; that's the mindset of the Scripture and what I want to teach you to do.

❖ Just announce freedom to the captives; that declaration should shake up the enemy to where demons start to vacate if they are there.

What happens to demons when the gospel message is announced?

_____

_____

_____

_____

_____

❖ <u>Isaiah 59:19 AMP:</u>

So they will fear the name of the Lord from the west and His glory from the rising of the sun. For He will come in like a narrow, rushing stream which the breath of the Lord drives [overwhelming the enemy].

- Isaiah 59:19 expresses that when the enemy comes in, like a flood, the Spirit of the Lord will raise up a standard against him.

- Some translations are unclear, making it sound like the enemy is the one who pursues us like a flood; however, the scripture expresses that when the enemy comes, the flood of the Spirit will come in and raise up a standard against that enemy.

- I want you to frame this right; in any situation you encounter, the Spirit of the Lord will raise up a standard. He will come in like a flood.

❖ Picture this—just as God flooded the earth to destroy the enemy in Genesis, He is flooding out your spiritual enemies. I encourage you to meditate on this revelation.

How does the Holy Spirit respond when the enemy comes against you, according to Isaiah 59:19?

_____

_____

_____

_____

_____

GOD IS A WARRIOR WHO SAVES

DISCUSSION:

God wants to train all of His people to speak by the Spirit, which is how everyone who believed in Jesus Christ spoke in the New Testament. Paul said everyone has a word, a psalm, a tongue, or an interpretation (1 Corinthians 14:26–33). He taught that it must be done in order, with those seated in the congregation judging whether the words spoken are of God. With that in mind, if you knew that the entire assembly could say yay or nay, would you stand up and deliver what you feel you're supposed to say? Are you strong enough in your Spirit about what you're about to do or say? Are you sure you would be able to withstand the judgment of the congregation? That's what Paul taught—everyone seated is to judge the words.

The Lord once said to me, "I am a warrior." I knew I had heard that in Scripture before, and soon found it in Zephaniah 3:17 AMP. This verse declares that the Lord God is in the midst of you as a mighty, victorious warrior who will save you. He will rejoice over you with joy and quiet you in His love. The revelation from this verse inspired us to name the ministry Warrior Notes. Zephaniah 3:17 is my favorite verse. The Lord sent someone to share the message of this verse with me when I first got saved.

In 1982, when I was in my second year of college, an unknown individual knocked on my door. He claimed to be a student, but was only there for one semester. I don't remember his name or previously seeing him, which was strange. I was fasting and praying when he knocked on the door. When I let him in, he stood there and told me the powerful message the Lord gave him. He said, "I saw the enemy surrounding you. Then I saw the Lord come up to you. He was riding a white horse and handed you a stone with the phrase 'victorious warrior' on it. Then the Lord rode off." He shared his vision and prophetic word, then walked out. I never saw him again. Though I tried to find his name, I couldn't locate him or find out anything about him. To this day, I don't know if he was actually a person or an angel.

I believe that message from the mysterious student was how Warrior Notes came to be. The Lord is the ultimate warrior, and I knew Warrior Notes would be a story about victory. That was my white stone, which I later found written about in the Bible. Revelation 2:17 states that those who overcome are given a white stone with their new name on it. I later realized the depth of what this person shared with me when he saw the Lord hand me a white stone with the words victorious warrior.

I encourage you to study Zephaniah 3:17 and meditate on it. I want to emphasize that God will save you from your enemies; He will rejoice over you with joy and quiet or comfort you in His love. He has songs of joy that He sings over you; some translations call them songs of deliverance. The Lord will sing songs of deliverance over you and around you, which is the flavor of what the young man saw in his vision. There were armies of enemies around me, which hemmed me in on every side. It didn't look like I had a chance. Then the Lord handed me that stone, and that was the end of the enemy. The Lord had decreed that I would have victory over the enemy.

Read and meditate on Zephaniah 3:17. What is God speaking to you from this verse and Dr. Zadai's testimony?

_____

_____

_____

_____

❖ Joel 2:11 KJV:

And the Lord shall utter His voice before His army: for His camp is very great: for He is strong that executeth His word: for the day of the Lord is great and very terrible; and who can abide it?

- Joel 2:11 is another verse I recommend memorizing.

- The heart of Warrior Notes is to train you to speak what the Spirit is saying, not what you think or feel.

- The Lord wants to speak through you as He utters His voice before His army.

- I picture all of us as ministers who communicate what the Spirit is saying, addressing the army of God.

- When I speak, I'm ministering to all of you chosen ones in the army of God.

- Even though I don't know everyone in the body of Christ on the earth now, as people join us, I'm discovering how expansive it is.

- Hundreds of thousands of people worldwide have connected to Warrior Notes. A couple of years ago, we would have never known that so many people have been educated and discipled by the Spirit of God.

- God is uniting His people so that we will essentially utter forth what God is saying, fulfilling Joel's prophecy.

What does Joel 2:11 prophesy? Who does God want to utter His voice through?

_____

_____

_____

_____

_____

❖ **Hebrews 1:14 AMP:**

Are not all the angels ministering spirits sent out [by God] to serve (accompany, protect) those who will inherit salvation? [Of course they are!]

- The Lord reminded me of the encounter from college when I received my ministry, Warrior Notes, and wrote my first book. I realized that everything God did was tied to this vision that the young man shared with me.

- Then, I came to understand that the angels also had a part in my fulfillment of God's will.

- When there's angelic activity, it hinders satan and evil spirits.

- These mighty angels have often accompanied me and aided in ministry. Even as I share this revelation with you, angels surround me, and the enemy doesn't stand a chance.

- I noticed that when I'm ministering, whether writing a book, filming, or teaching at a conference, those angels come and help rout the enemy out.

- Sometimes demons just leave, even if I didn't fast or address them, as you would think. The angelic visitation somehow caused a deliverance.

- A person may fast or pray for deliverance, but sometimes, it doesn't happen as expected; it often comes through angelic activity.

What is the role of angels in a believer's life? And what often comes as a result of angelic activity?

_____

_____

_____

_____

_____

CHAPTER 9

THE LORD'S ANGELIC ARMY

O Lord God of Heaven's Armies! Where is there anyone as mighty as You, O Lord? You are entirely faithful.
—Psalm 89:8 NLT

DISCUSSION:

Throughout church history, we have been trying to figure out the working mode for ministry, including deliverance. We have tried one method for a while, then switched to another. One moment, people were told to let go, and then, in the next, they were instructed to hold on. Many deliverance ministries have people cough and do all these forced manifestations to try to make it work. Like deliverance, ministries have devised many fleshly modes of getting people filled with the Holy Spirit. You should let the power of God come on a person and fill them with the Spirit; He doesn't need help. In the early church, ministers did not coerce people, pat them on the back, or tell them to speak a specific word in tongues. People have been filled with the Spirit and weren't even instructed to speak in tongues.

In the book of Acts, there are several instances where people were filled with the Spirit; in all but one occurrence, people started speaking in tongues. There was only one time where it didn't specify that they spoke in tongues, but it's inferred that they did (Acts 8:15–17). In all the other passages, they clearly spoke in tongues when filled with the Spirit. The apostles explained to people that they needed to be filled with the Spirit, which is a different experience than salvation. They weren't told that they would speak in tongues—they just did, which makes it more profound (Acts 2:4; 10:44–46). So, if people were filled with the Spirit without being told they needed to speak in tongues, why are ministries operating the way they do today? Many deliverance ministers ask people to do and say unbiblical things. They even talk to the demons instead of those receiving ministry, pushing for a manifestation. In the Bible days, demons spoke up; they were so freaked out and frustrated by the presence of Jesus or those He sent out that they just manifested.

We briefly discussed angelic activity in the last chapter and will continue to dive deeper into understanding how angels aid with deliverance. God can do what He wants but never goes against His Word. In the Bible, one can discover how God established the realms, with angels involved in warfare.

Why is it dangerous for ministries to figure out "methods" for activities that can only be accomplished by God's supernatural power?

_____
_____
_____
_____
_____

❖ **Joshua 5:13–14 AMP:**

Now when Joshua was by Jericho, he looked up, and behold, a man was standing opposite him with his drawn sword in his hand, and Joshua went to him and said to him, "Are you for us or for our adversaries?" He said, "No; rather I have come now as captain of the army of the Lord." Then Joshua fell with his face toward the earth and bowed down, and said to him, "What does my lord have to say to his servant?"

- In Joshua 5, the angel of the Lord approached Joshua, who was already in warfare mode.

- When encountering this warrior on the road, he had just led the Israelites toward Jerusalem, conquering cities with hybrid giants.

- Joshua thought he was flesh and blood and was ready to fight as he asked, "Are you for us or against us?" He wasn't afraid because he was sent. The angel of the Lord surprisingly replied, "Neither."

- He was completely neutral, neither for nor against anyone, but came as the captain of the Lord's army.

- It is a profound statement that the angel of the Lord wasn't taking sides with Joshua or anyone else; he was on the Lord's side and was also sent.

- The Lord had sent His army to help but did not tell Joshua at first.

- The commander angel had to wait for God's instruction; however, it didn't come through Joshua.

- Interestingly, many ministries attempt to define everything and to set up plans that do not work.

Describe how the angel conducted himself in Joshua 5:13–14. Did he act on his own accord?

_____

_____

_____

_____

_____

❖ <u>Luke 10:17–20:</u>

> Then the seventy returned with joy, saying, "Lord, even the demons are subject to us in Your name." And He said to them, "I saw satan fall like lightning from heaven. Behold, I give you the authority to trample on serpents and scorpions, and over all the power of the enemy, and nothing shall by any means hurt you. Nevertheless do not rejoice in this, that the spirits are subject to you, but rather rejoice because your names are written in heaven."

- According to some translations, the seventy (or seventy-two) Jesus sent out in Luke 10 were surprised that the demons obeyed them.

- Jesus told his followers not to rejoice because they cast out demons, but rejoice because their names were written in the Lamb's Book of Life.

- In other words, we are not supposed to focus on the fact that demons obey us; our focus should be on our salvation and that we are ambassadors.

- This passage is recorded because of the abuse Jesus knew would occur in the coming days.

- I will not conjure up a manifestation or implement a mode of operation based on what the devil does because anything he says or does is a lie.

- You can't trust the devil with anything; he can quote Scripture better than you can and will try to twist God's Word.

- You can't depend upon anything a demon says. Why would you want to talk to them if they're liars anyway? Even if they did say something true, how would you know?

Why did Jesus tell His followers not to rejoice that they cast out demons? What were they to rejoice in?

_____
_____
_____
_____
_____

Why shouldn't you talk to demons?

_____
_____
_____
_____
_____

❖ **1 Peter 4:10-11 ESV:**

As each has received a gift, use it to serve one another, as good stewards of God's varied grace: whoever speaks, as one who speaks oracles of God; whoever serves, as one who serves by the strength that God supplies—in order that in everything God may be glorified through Jesus Christ. To Him belong glory and dominion forever and ever. Amen.

- The standard of ministry in the New Testament is not how it operates today. We are not as effective because we have veered from God's way.

- Too many ministers are looking for manifestations with a method so that they can call it their ministry.

- The last time I checked, it was the ministry of the Holy Spirit—the ministry of Jesus through us—not our ministry.

- If we are going to speak, we must speak by the Spirit.

- We must also address the enemy the way the Spirit of God would address demons.

- The Lord in our midst is a victorious warrior; He has defeated the enemy.

- The only reason the enemy obeys us is because of Jesus Christ, not us.

- That's why Jesus said not to rejoice when the enemy listens to you, but rejoice that your names are written in Heaven. Who wrote your name there? Jesus did.

❖ Jesus wrote our names in the Lamb's Book of Life because He purchased us long ago (1 Corinthians 6:20). The demons obey us solely for this reason, not because we're spiritual or to be feared.

❖ The enemy knows who we are, but obeys us only because we're associated with Jesus Christ. We all must remember this.

What is the only reason that demons obey us? Why do we need to remember this?

_____

_____

_____

_____

ANGELS WAR ON OUR BEHALF

DISCUSSION:

Sometimes, when angels show up, we can step into a new place, just like what happened with Joshua. Joshua was moving into new territory when he met the captain of the Lord's army and didn't even discern that it was an angel. At first, he thought it was a human being confronting him. The angel was not taking sides but following the Lord's instruction. Angels encamp around us and do the Lord's bidding, hearkening unto His voice. Their arrival sometimes causes instant deliverance.

❖ **Psalm 103:20:**

Bless the Lord, you His angels, who excel in strength, who do His word, heeding the voice of His word.

- Angel activity can cause the enemy to be routed.

- Sometimes, when angels work, you don't have an inkling of what happened; you wouldn't be able to explain it or create a seminar. All you'd know is that the enemy's eyes suddenly got big, and he ran off.

- We would never want to take credit for this because the Lord Jesus Christ sends angels to surround us which results in deliverance.

- Although I often witness angelic activity, I want to see more of it in all of our lives. God intervenes in ways far too wonderful for it to ever come from us.

According to Psalm 103:20, what do angels respond to?

_____

_____

_____

_____

_____

❖ **Psalms 34:7:**

The angel of the Lord encamps around those who fear Him, and delivers them.

- The angel encamps around the people who fear the Lord.

- That's your job—to fear the Lord—and the angel gets the credit for encamping around you.

- You hardly hear any teaching about the fear of the Lord; however, the fear of the Lord brings the angel in to deliver you.

- Psalms 34:7 mentions one singular angel, just as the captain of the host of the Lord's army was just one being in Joshua 5:13-15. He was the head commander of the angelic host of Heaven.

- The captain of the Lord's army may even be Jesus Himself, which is what I believe. This was implied when I was in Heaven, although I was not explicitly shown it was Him. It's not defined in the Bible whether or not the captain of the host is Jesus, but I felt that He was when I was there.

- Always remember that the angel of the Lord encamps around those who fear Him.

How do angels respond to those who fear the Lord? Why is it essential for us to stay humble?

_____

_____

_____

_____

_____

❖ **2 Kings 6:16 KJV:**
  And he answered, Fear not: for they that be with us are more than they that be with them.

- These military angels are sent to encompass you and are ministering spirits sent forth to minister for those who will inherit salvation (Hebrews 1:14).

- When I was in Heaven, Jesus shared a very profound statement with me: Everyone was purchased; there wasn't one human being that wasn't redeemed through His blood.

- Everyone was destined by God, who wrote their books and planned for them to come to the knowledge of Jesus Christ. However, most people on earth do not understand their destiny.

- Even though the price was paid and the angels were sent to minister to people destined to inherit salvation, many still reject the Lord and go to hell. Yet, their books are written as though they go to Heaven.

- The angels do not take sides with individuals; they only do the will of the Father.

- Jesus showed me that angels were sent to unsaved people to bring them to a place of the knowledge of God. They lead them to a place where people preach the gospel and mentor them, hoping they get saved.

- These angels are the ones sent to minister for those who are going to inherit salvation (Hebrews 1:14); it's preemptive, on credit.

❖ In other words, before people are saved, the angels are told to minister to them. They are to lead them to situations where they can encounter the truth. For example, an angel may bring someone in your path so that you can talk to them or that God can meet their need, providing through you.

What percentage of people did Jesus intend for salvation? How do angels work with unsaved people to bring them to salvation?

_____

_____

_____

_____

_____

❖ John 14:6:

Jesus said to him, "I am the way, the truth, and the life. No one comes to the Father except through Me."

- God keeps unsaved people safe from all kinds of situations where they would have died before they could accept salvation; this is the truth.

- Jesus said that He treats people as though they're coming to Heaven; the angels are also instructed that way.

- This truth is not widely accepted, but the Lord sees everyone as coming to be with Him because He purchased all humanity.

- That means that everyone has the chance to accept Jesus Christ.

- If they accept Him as the way, they enter into the kingdom of God; if not, they will not enter in.

How do Jesus and the angels treat every single person?

_____

_____

_____

_____

INSTANT DELIVERANCE

DISCUSSION:

My question is, with what has been offered to us in the Scriptures, why do we depend so much on alternatives for our deliverance? We have so much help offered to us and so many benefits from God. I believe that we settle for counterfeits because we don't know the truth. I used to seek others out to pray over me for deliverance and to deal with the devil; in some instances, it helped, yet I noticed it wasn't permanent. It was temporary because the truth hadn't become a part of me. The reality of my deliverance hadn't been fortified with the Word of God.

To maintain my deliverance, I learned that I needed to fill my house with the Word of God so that my spiritual being grew more powerful. The Lord once showed me how big my inner man was in the spirit; I was much bigger, like a giant, in the spirit in comparison to my body. Back when I was in the operating room, and the Lord appeared to me and took me to Heaven, He showed me that I had developed my spiritual walk with Him so that the sphere of influence of my spirit reached a circumference of thirty feet if I stood in the middle.

Jesus also showed me the apostle Lester Sumrall, whose spiritual proximity was the size of the entire city of San Francisco. When

Brother Sumrall went there and other cities, the demons would be arrested. To prevent being cast out, they intentionally left town before he arrived so they wouldn't come under his authority. The demons thought that if they went on their own, when Brother Sumrall left the city, they would be able to return; however, if addressed by Him, they would have to obey. The Lord showed me that when he went into the city of San Francisco, the evil spirits came under his authority and were paralyzed. Entire regions were affected by his presence.

❖ <u>Romans 16:20 KJV:</u>

And the God of peace shall bruise satan under your feet shortly. The grace of our Lord Jesus Christ be with you. Amen.

- Luke 10:19 talks about believers trampling on the serpents and scorpions, having power and authority over all the enemy.

- In Romans 16:20, Paul specifically mentioned that satan would shortly be bruised under the feet of the Roman congregation that he addressed in this letter.

- He said they would bruise satan; he would be under their feet shortly. That was a word that God gave Paul for them.

- We address the enemy the same way today.

What does Romans 16:20 say that the God of peace will do to the enemy? Whose feet will God crush him under?

_____

_____

_____

_____

_____

We must believe that no matter what harassment we're going through with the enemy, it's just a matter of time before we crush satan under our feet; this word is for us, too.

❖ <u>Psalms 32:7 KJV:</u>

Thou art my hiding place; Thou shalt preserve me from trouble; Thou shalt compass me about with songs of deliverance. Selah.

- Psalm 32:7 promises that we are preserved because God provides a hiding place to protect us from trouble.

- There is a fortress that God gives as a hiding place that you can run into; it will keep you from danger.

- As He promised in Zephaniah 3:17, He will surround you, encompassing you with songs of deliverance. God Himself will sing over you.

- I have awakened at night and heard the Lord singing songs of deliverance over me. Because of the Lord's protection through these songs, the enemy couldn't operate against me or even touch me.

- Eventually, the hiding place became permanent, which is what the Lord wants to do for you, too.

- This promise is not just for me; it's in the Bible and is available to everybody. We all can take the words of the Bible as our own.

In Psalm 32:7, what does the psalmist mean by saying God is his hiding place?

_____
_____
_____
_____
_____

You must expect the Lord to provide that hiding place for you, mentioned in Psalm 32:7, and instruct you on how to get there. Once you are in there, you're preserved from trouble, period. That would be enough for me, but He adds that He will encompass you.

When God sings these songs about deliverance over and around you, the enemy will leave you because the Lord is essentially prophesying over you. When He speaks, it's a done deal; the enemy knows that. When God surrounds you this way, there is instant deliverance.

How can you make God your permanent hiding place?

_____
_____
_____
_____
_____

CHAPTER 10

God Is Your Deliverer

How God anointed Jesus of Nazareth with the Holy Spirit and with power, who went about doing good and healing all who were oppressed by the devil, for God was with Him.
—Acts 10:38

DISCUSSION:

I want to note that the Holy Spirit is said to have led Jesus into the desert to be tempted by the devil. This leading sounds strange to many of us because of how we've been taught; it's contrary to the mindset that many of us have about God. Matthew 4:1–11 talks about the temptation of Jesus where the Holy Spirit actually set up a confrontation between Him and the devil. Jesus had to combat with the devil as the Son of Man; He did not wage war as the Son of God. Acts 10:38 clearly expresses that He was Jesus of Nazareth, who was anointed by the Holy Spirit and went around doing good, healing everyone who was oppressed by the devil because God was with Him.

- ❖ Matthew 4:1:

    Then Jesus was led up by the Spirit into the wilderness to be tempted by the devil.

    - Jesus was just obeying as He was led into the desert and went face-to-face with the devil.

    - When satan addressed Him, Jesus didn't respond as the Son of God; He responded as a servant sent by God and anointed by the Holy Spirit (Philippians 2:6–8).

- Jesus did this for us without needing to prove anything.

- He is the One who created helel, the angel who became corrupted that we now call satan. After the fall, he came to be known as lucifer, the god of this world who stole the human race from God through Adam and Eve.

❖ <u>Philippians 2:5–9 NLT:</u>

You must have the same attitude that Christ Jesus had. Though He was God, He did not think of equality with God as something to cling to. Instead, He gave up His divine privileges; He took the humble position of a slave and was born as a human being. When He appeared in human form, He humbled Himself in obedience to God and died a criminal's death on a cross. Therefore, God elevated Him to the place of highest honor and gave Him the name above all other names.

- Jesus went into the desert as a human being; He was God in a body but lived as a servant.

- Philippians 2:6–7 explains that He laid aside His Godhead ability, considering equality with God as nothing.

- That's what the Scriptures say.

- Jesus did not operate as a deity but as one who serves.

- He lived and ministered as the anointed Person called the Son of Man, which is controversial yet true.

❖ When Jesus encountered demons, they recognized Him and said, "You are the Son of God." He told them to shut up because He wanted to be known as the Son of Man.

❖ When He was in the desert, satan confronted Him as the Son of God; however, Jesus responded as the Son of Man. The temptation was satan trying to get Jesus to operate as the Son of God, which He wasn't allowed to do.

Why was it so important that Jesus did everything as the Son of Man, not the Son of God?

_____

_____

_____

_____

_____

❖ **John 14:12 NLT:**

   I tell you the truth, anyone who believes in Me will do the same works I have done, and even greater works, because I am going to be with the Father.

- Jesus lived on the earth as a servant.

- After He was crucified and resurrected, He taught the disciples to live the same way, encouraging them that they would do even greater works because He was going to the Father (John 14:12).

- Jesus had to accomplish the Father's will as a human under the guidance, power, and anointing of the Holy Spirit so that He could transfer His ministry to His body, which is all of us on the earth.

- This was the plan of God, and satan knew it, so he tried to throw Him off track by saying, "If you are the Son of God, do this."

- In other words, satan challenged Jesus by saying if you really are who you claim to be, then prove it.

- What satan asked Jesus to do in the wilderness was out of bounds of what He was permitted to do as a human, so he refused.

- Jesus resisted the temptations to act as the Son of God by telling satan no and deferring to the Father.

- He replied to all three temptations, saying, "It is written" (Matthew 4:4, 7, 10).

- Every time satan demanded a miracle, Jesus countered his words; He refused to jump off a building or turn a rock into bread.

- Jesus wouldn't give in to these temptations because they were meant to get Him out of God's boundaries.

- The bottom line is that we are to do the same.

- If Jesus used the Word of God to combat the devil, then that's what we need to do as well.

❖ We are supposed to respond to the enemy just like Jesus did by deferring to the words that came out of God's mouth.

In John 14:12, what does Jesus say those who believe in Him will do?

_____
_____
_____
_____
_____

How are we supposed to respond to the enemy's lies and temptations?

_____
_____
_____
_____
_____

GOD'S WORD COMBATS THE ENEMY

DISCUSSION:

You don't need to pay somebody to train or deliver you; however, at times you need help because you're so overwhelmed and have allowed the enemy to come in. That's where the body of Christ can help. Yet, must you seek out a special minister for deliverance? We don't see Paul charging for deliverance or even ministering it. He did not come to cast demons out of Timothy; he had already released a prophetic utterance, then instructed him to take those words and beat up the devil. Paul charged Timothy to start fighting with his prophecies. He didn't need to lay hands on him, address the devil, break demonic powers, and all these methods that we think we need a deliverance minister to do. Paul essentially told Timothy, "You have the weapons (which were prophecies), just use them."

❖ **1 Timothy 1:18 KJV:**

This charge I commit unto thee, son Timothy, according to the prophecies which went before on thee, that thou by them mightiest war a good warfare.

- In 1 Timothy 1:18, Paul reminded Timothy of the prophecies spoken over him.

- I believe that Paul delivered those words before Timothy, meaning they were looking forward.

- These prophetic utterances had to do with his future. Paul instructed him to use them as weapons of warfare.

- We should take prophecies as the word of the Lord and declare them in response to the enemy.

- You can establish the framework of what God is saying to you about your future by proclaiming forward-looking utterances; allow them to go before you.

- Use those weapons you've been given—prophetic words—to wage war against the enemy.

- Even if we have not received a prophetic message from someone, we should be using the Word of God prophetically to wage war on our own.

What did Paul tell Timothy to do with the prophecies he had been given? How do you wage war with prophecy?

_____

_____

_____

_____

_____

❖ 2 Timothy 1:6:

Therefore I remind you to stir up the gift of God which is in you through the laying on of my hands.

- In 2 Timothy 1:6, Paul charged Timothy to stir up the gift that he received by the laying on of hands and fan it into flame.

- In other words, it had gone out. What was once a fire became like hot coals; maybe it was smoking and had some heat, but he needed to fan it into flame.

- The effectiveness of a spiritual gift or impartation has to do with how the individual stewards it. Timothy needed to take action.

- Again, the question is, "Did Timothy need another word?" No. He needed to take the words he already received and wage war with them; that was enough.

- It works the same with the giftings. How often do you need hands laid on you before you are satisfied with your gifting? Your gifting is inside you and predestined from the foundations of the world (Ephesians 1:4–6; Romans 11:29).

What are we responsible for doing with the gifts that God has given us?

_____

_____

_____

_____

_____

DISCUSSION:

Everything we are meant to obtain in Christ was already predestined before the foundations of the world. The plans for your life were written before you were born (Psalm 139:16). Salvation was already established before Jesus hung on the cross; Revelation 13:8 says that He was the Lamb slain before the foundations of the world. God already saw Him slain before He created the universe. All the good works we were created to do were predestined in Christ. Even though people still go to hell, there are good works written in their books that they were supposed to do. Nobody needs to go to hell, but people still do.

There is so much written about you that has yet to be done. You should see how thick your book is and how little is done compared to the potential. In Heaven, Jesus showed me that I was operating at 35 percent, yet I had so much education and experience. I experienced multiple supernatural encounters, even before I went to Heaven. I attended the best ministerial schools and had almost every general that you can name lay hands on me. I sat under many great ministers, had their anointing come upon me in their meetings, and even received prophesies from some of them.

Despite all that happened to me, it didn't get me past 35 percent of what I could have done; the deficit was 65 percent. I was only doing about one-third of what was written about me. When I discovered how little I had done with what I had been given, I sincerely told Jesus I would have done so much more if I had known. Jesus said nothing to me, but the Holy Spirit said, "You could have known." I then knew it was my responsibility, and the conversation was over. If I said anything else, I would get myself in trouble because it was my fault, not God's.

❖ Although you may have experienced many disadvantages, your reward in Heaven is based only on what you were given. God is looking for you to produce a return on what He has placed in you.

What is our reward in Heaven based on?

_____

_____

_____

_____

_____

❖ 1 Peter 2:9 ESV:

But you are a chosen race, a royal priesthood, a holy nation, a people for His own possession, that you may proclaim the excellencies of Him who called you out of darkness into His marvelous light.

- We have all experienced a measure of deliverance because we were delivered from the kingdom of darkness into the kingdom of light.

- We used to obey this prince of the power of the air, but we no longer do because we now have the ability to resist him (Ephesians 2:1–3).

- When we were lost, we couldn't say no to satan, the god of this world; we were powerless and strictly obedient to him.

- Deliverance is being rescued from spiritual darkness and experiencing salvation by being born-again.

- That same resurrection power that rose Jesus from the dead delivered and translated you.

- You have already been transferred into God's kingdom of light.

How does 1 Peter 2:9 describe the people of God? How does this verse depict deliverance?

_____
_____
_____
_____
_____

A FILLED HOUSE KEEPS DEMONS OUT

DISCUSSION:

There are certain circumstances where you need somebody else to pray for you because the enemy just overcomes you. However, when you need other people to pray for you all the time, it means the results are not permanent. I understand that you can receive true deliverance from ministers. My wife, Kathi, was permanently delivered by receiving ministry from an individual, but she didn't seek it; she was just in the meeting and was called out by the gifts of the Spirit. She was already saved when this person addressed an evil spirit that was harassing her, and it never came back. Kathi filled herself with the Word of God, and that place was occupied by the Holy Spirit and the Word, which is why it was permanent.

How did Dr. Zadai's wife, Kathi, experience deliverance?

_____

_____

_____

_____

❖ <u>Matthew 12:43–45:</u>

When an unclean spirit goes out of a man, he goes through dry places, seeking rest, and finds none. Then he says, "I will return to my house from which I came." And when he comes, he finds it empty, swept, and put in order. Then he goes out and takes with him seven other spirits more wicked than himself, and they enter and dwell there; and the last state of that man is worse than the first. So shall it also be with this wicked generation.

- Concerning deliverance, Jesus taught that when you cast out a demon, it leaves and goes to an arid, desert place.

- This is difficult for the evil spirit because it wants to return to where it lived.

- When that unclean spirit returns, it finds the person swept clean, which is what sometimes happens in deliverance.

- The key in Matthew 12:43–45 is that the person was found empty or unoccupied.

- The passage doesn't specify if the person had ever been filled with the Holy Spirit; the bottom line was the evil spirit could come back if that individual was not currently occupied with the Spirit and the Word of God filling up their house.

- If they were empty, the evil spirit would then find other disembodied spirits to come back with it, leaving the person seven times worse than their original condition.

❖ You must remember that if you cast a devil out of a person, they need to be discipled and mentored in the Word of God and the Holy Spirit so that their house is filled; that way, the evil spirit will not be able to return. This is the whole message behind what Jesus said in Matthew 12:43–45, where He made deliverance easy.

❖ Today, most deliverance ministries focus on casting demons out of people, yet they are not fathering or mentoring. This may not go over well, but it's not helping anybody just to cast the devil out. Based on what we see today, many have ignored Jesus's teaching.

What is the message Jesus taught in Matthew 12:43–45? How does a person keep their "house" filled?

_____
_____
_____
_____
_____

What is missing from many deliverance ministries today? Why is the lack of mentoring dangerous for the person receiving deliverance?

_____
_____
_____
_____
_____

DISCUSSION:

My concern regarding deliverance ministry is not just what happens today, but the person's well-being tomorrow. In other words, if I address the devil in your life and drive him out, have I done the fathering and mentoring for you to maintain your freedom? Have I provided you with the tools to fill you up and to allow the Holy Spirit to occupy you so completely that the evil spirit can't come back in? I would want you to stay free, like my wife, Kathi. Most people end up worse off if they're not mentored and filled with the Holy Spirit and the Word of God. You must have the Scriptures in your arsenal to combat the enemy like Jesus did in Matthew 4; your deliverance must be sealed.

I am called to be a father, not just a teacher (1 Corinthians 4:15). The best way for me to father and mentor you is by sharing the truth through books and media; we have thousands and thousands of people, which makes it difficult to provide individual mentorship. I want you to be in a class of warriors where you experience deliverance because the Lord comes to you and sings songs over you (Zephaniah 3:17).

Wage war with the prophecies that have been given to you and fan your gifts into flame so that you don't have to depend on others (1 Timothy 1:18; 2 Timothy 1:6). Even though the body of Christ is there for us, we shouldn't focus on individuals as being our answer. Paul essentially taught Timothy that everything he needed had been given; now he just had to fan it into flame and wage war with his prophecies; he had to grow up. The bottom line is that every one of us has to mature at some point.

- ❖ **Hebrews 4:12 NLT:**

    For the Word of God is alive and powerful. It is sharper than the sharpest two-edged sword, cutting between soul and spirit, between joint and marrow. It exposes our innermost thoughts and desires.

- ❖ **Ephesians 6:16–17:**

    Above all, taking the shield of faith with which you will be able to quench all the fiery darts of the wicked one. And take the helmet of salvation, and the sword of the Spirit, which is the Word of God.

    - The Word of God is a weapon—the sword of the Spirit—that cuts in, dividing that which is of the soul and the spirit.

- When the enemy tries to come back or attack you, you must have the shield of faith; your faith must be built up to extinguish every lie from the enemy.

- Remember that you have all of these tools; when you know how to use your weapons, deliverance becomes very simple.

How can you use the Word of God as your weapon, according to Hebrews 4:12 and Ephesians 6:16–17?

_____

_____

_____

_____

_____

❖ Psalms 34:17:

The righteous cry out, and the Lord hears, and delivers them out of all their troubles.

❖ Psalm 107:6:

Then they cried out to the Lord in their trouble, and He delivered them out of their distresses.

❖ Psalm 50:15:

Call upon Me in the day of trouble; I will deliver you, and you shall glorify Me.

What does the Lord promise to do for those who cry out to Him?

_____

_____

_____

_____

DISCUSSION:

Let's get back to the simplicity of deliverance. When you cry for help, the Lord hears and delivers you out of your trouble and distress; the Scriptures do not imply that it involves other individuals, even though we have each other. Psalms 50:15 says that you will call on the Lord in the day of trouble, and He will deliver you; you will glorify Him, not give credit to other people. God is your Deliverer. We need to get back to the basics.

You have been set on the path for permanent deliverance; then you will cause others to be set free, and it will last in their lives, too. Why? Because you will disciple people, which leads to lasting breakthroughs. Through mentorship, they will be occupied by the truth and the Holy Spirit.

A PRAYER FOR YOU

Father, thank You for giving us the authority to drive out the enemy in the name of Jesus and through the power of His blood. Thank You for every reader receiving their deliverance as You sing songs over them and send Your angels to encamp around them. Thank You for the Messiah's anointing, breaking the yokes off of people permanently. Lord, I pray that You also turn their testimonies into deliverance for others. I declare that they are Your ambassadors who carry deliverance with them. Father, confirm Your word with signs and wonders following, in the name of Jesus, amen.

Salvation Prayer

Lord God,
I confess that I am a sinner.
I confess that I need Your Son, Jesus.
Please forgive me in His name.
Lord Jesus, I believe You died for me and that You
are alive and listening to me now.
I now turn from my sins and welcome
You into my heart. Come and take control of my life.
Make me the kind of person You want me to be.
Now, fill me with Your Holy Spirit, who
will show me how to live for You.
I acknowledge You before men as my Savior and my Lord.
In Jesus' name. Amen.

IF YOU PRAYED THIS PRAYER,
PLEASE GET IN TOUCH WITH US AT

info@kevinzadai.com

We welcome you to join our network at
Warriornotes.tv for access to exclusive programming.

To enroll in our ministry school, go to:
www.Warriornotesschool.com

Visit **www.KevinZadai.com** for
additional ministry materials.

ABOUT
DR. KEVIN ZADAI

Kevin Zadai, Th.D., was called to the ministry at the age of ten. He attended Central Bible College in Springfield, Missouri, where he received a Bachelor of Arts in theology. Later, he received training in missions at Rhema Bible College and a Th.D. at Primus University. Dr. Kevin L. Zadai is dedicated to training Christians to live and operate in two realms at once— the supernatural and the natural.

At age thirty-one, Kevin met Jesus in Heaven, got a second chance at life, and received a revelation that he could not fail because it's all rigged in our favor! Kevin holds a commercial pilot license and is retired from Southwest Airlines after twenty-nine years as a flight attendant. He is the founder and president of Warrior Notes School of Ministry. He and his lovely wife, Kathi, reside in New Orleans, Louisiana.

Check It Out!
These Other Recent Study Guides
by Dr. Kevin Zadai

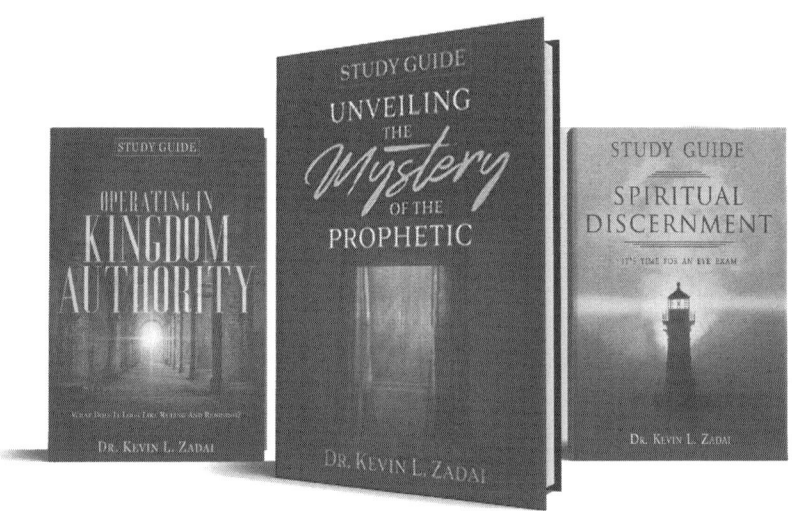

Operating In Kingdom Authority — Study Guide

Unveiling The Mystery of The Prophetic — Study Guide

Spiritual Discernment: It's Time For An Eye Exam — Study Guide

Kevin has written over
sixty-five books and study guides.

Please see our website for a complete list of materials.

www.Kevinzadai.com